qp

Louisiana Civil Law Dictionary

Gregory W. Rome
Stephan Kinsella

qp

Quid Pro Books
New Orleans, Louisiana

Louisiana Civil Law Dictionary

Published in 2011 by Quid Pro Books.

ISBN-13 9781610270816
ISBN 1610270819

Quid Pro, LLC

5860 Citrus Blvd., Suite D-101
New Orleans, Louisiana 70123
www.quidprobooks.com

This book is also available in quality ebook editions from leading digital booksellers. For all bulk orders, school adoptions, review copies, and information about available ebook formats and classroom uses, please contact the publisher at info@quidprobooks.com.

Reader suggestions are welcome. Please write to the authors via email: gwrome@williamsandrome.com. Of course, the information and opinions expressed in this dictionary are for educational and professional purposes and do not constitute legal advice or the practice of law. Information about the authors' practices appears at the end of this book.

Publisher's Cataloging-in-Publication

Rome, Gregory W.; Kinsella, Stephan.
    Louisiana civil law dictionary / Gregory W. Rome and Stephan Kinsella.
       p. cm.
    ISBN: 1610270819 (pbk)
1. Law—United States—Dictionaries. 2. Civil law system. 3. Legal research—Louisiana. I. Title.
KF155.R493 2011
349.7301'2—dc22
CIP

Contents

To my parents, Sharon Williams and Claude Rome,
and to Professor Yiannopoulos.

−− GWR

To Saúl Litvinoff, and also to A.N. Yiannopoulos.

−− SK

Louisiana
Civil Law
Dictionary

Preface

Unlike the legal systems of her forty-nine common law sister states, Louisiana's unique regime is largely based on the civil law. Not surprisingly, Louisiana's civilian system employs concepts and vocabulary significantly different from those of the federal legal system and of the other states' common law systems. As Professor Shael Herman notes:

> A lawyer from elsewhere in the United States could not expect to understand [the Louisiana Civil Code's] vocabulary just because he had studied law. This is so because the Louisiana Civil Code, unlike any other lawbook in force in the United States, employs the terminology and conceptions of French and Spanish law, both heavily indebted to Roman law.[1]

For this reason, American common law attorneys are wary of legal dealings involving Louisiana. In Louisiana-based lawsuits and transactions, they can encounter unfamiliar terms like emphyteusis, naked ownership, usufruct, virile portions, vulgar substitutions, synallagmatic contracts, falcidian portions, mystic testaments, antichresis, whimsical conditions, and lesion beyond moiety. Even many Louisiana-trained attorneys are unfamiliar with terms like amicable compounder, jactitation, mutuum, and commodatum. And because of the strong influence of the dominant federal and state common law systems surrounding Louisiana, common law terms are often employed informally in Louisiana. For example, the common law term *stare decisis* is often used erroneously in Louisiana, instead of *jurisprudence constante*. This contributes to confusion as to which term is accurate.

To address such concerns, we compiled this dictionary of civil law words and phrases to serve as a convenient reference for the benefit of students, scholars, legal secretaries, paralegals, notaries, and of course practicing attorneys—in Louisiana and common law

---

[1] SHAEL HERMAN, THE LOUISIANA CIVIL CODE: A EUROPEAN LEGACY FOR THE UNITED STATES 9 (1993). For useful discussions of the civil code and its history in Louisiana, see *ibid.*, and A.N. Yiannopoulos, *The Civil Codes of Louisiana*, 1 CIV. L. COMMENTARIES 1 (2008), http://www.law.tulane.edu/tlscenters/eason/index.aspx?id=12946. A good summary of the history of the legal systems of both Louisiana and Texas (as a representative common law state) can also be found in Patrick H. Martin & J. Lanier Yeates, *Louisiana and Texas Oil and Gas Law: An Overview of the Differences*, 52 LA. L. REV. 769, 769–782 (1992).

jurisdictions, as well as the many civil law jurisdictions in other countries. It is a greatly expanded, updated, and improved version of a law review article published in 1994 by one of the authors,[2] which was itself originally inspired by his repeated experience of explaining and translating Louisiana legal terminology to common law colleagues in a Houston law firm. We hope you find it useful.

GREGORY W. ROME
Chalmette, Louisiana

STEPHAN KINSELLA
Houston, Texas

March 2011

---

[2] Stephan Kinsella, *A Civil Law to Common Law Dictionary*, 54 LA. L. REV. 1265 (1994).

A Note on Usage

Terms printed in SMALL CAPS are discussed in separate entries. For example, in the dictionary entry for "servient estate," one discovers that it is the land burdened by a PREDIAL SERVITUDE. The small caps signal that there is also an entry for "predial servitude," should the reader need more information.

Most entries refer to relevant code articles or statutes. To conserve space, we have used abbreviated citations for statutes and codes. A table of the abbreviations follows at the end of this section. All citations without a specific date in the citation are current as of 2011 and refer to the current version of the West's annotated Louisiana materials. Occasionally, an entry refers to an older version of the code, and the year of that code is noted in parentheses. Wherever possible, primary sources are cited.

Note also that some of the Louisiana expressions discussed in this dictionary are commonly used in other states. The phrase "immovable property," for example, has been used in Texas statutes.[3] And, as noted above, common law terminology is used increasingly in Louisiana, as a result of the influence of Louisiana's sister states, in notable situations in which civilian terminology properly belongs (such as the use of *stare decisis* instead of *jurisprudence constante*).

Abbreviation	Full Citation
La. C.C. art.	La. Civil Code Annotated art.
La. C.C.P. art.	La. Code of Civil Procedure Annotated art.
La. R.S.	La. Revised Statutes Annotated

---

[3] TEX. INS. CODE ANN. art. 21.49, § 3(f) provides: "'Insurable property' means immovable property at fixed locations in a catastrophe area or corporeal movable property located therein...." *See also* TEX. R. CIV. P. 695, entitled "No receiver of immovable property appointed without notice."

A

Absolute simulation. *See* SIMULATION, ABSOLUTE SIMULATION.

Abuse of right. A doctrine providing "that 'fault' in the DELICTUAL sense may be imposed upon a party who has exercised a right in a manner that has caused injury to another." George M. Armstrong, Jr., & John C. LaMaster, *Retaliatory Eviction as Abuse of Rights: A Civilian Approach to Landlord-Tenant Disputes*, 47 LA. L. REV. 1, 15 (1986). *See* La. C.C. arts. 667–669; *Higgins Oil & Fuel Co. v. Guaranty Oil Co.*, 82 So. 206 (La. 1919) (abuse of rights of ownership).

> To justify the application of the doctrine of "abuse of rights," one of the following must exist: (1) the exercise of rights exclusively for the purpose of harming another or with the predominant motive to cause harm; (2) the non-existence of a serious and legitimate interest that is worthy of judicial protection; (3) the use of the right in violation of moral rules, good faith or elementary fairness; or (4) the exercise of the right for a purpose other than that for which it was granted.

210 Baronne St. Ltd. Partnership v. First Nat'l Bank of Commerce, 543 So.2d 502, 507 (La. App. 4 Cir. 1989), writ denied, 546 So.2d 1219.

Accession. The right by which the owner of a THING owns the FRUITS and PRODUCTS of that thing and anything attached to it. La. C.C. art. 482. *See* La. C.C. arts. 483–516; *see, also,* ALLUVION and DERELICTION.

Accretion. An accumulation, growth, or increase.

> **Accretion of a renounced succession.** The devolution of "rights of an INTESTATE SUCCESSOR who renounces ... to those persons who would have succeeded to them if the [renouncing] successor had predeceased the decedent." La. C.C. art. 964. Similarly, a LEGACY accretes to those persons who would have received it had a renouncing TESTATE

SUCCESSOR predeceased the TESTATOR, subject to any governing language in the will. La. C.C. art. 965.

Accretion on the banks of rivers and streams. *See* ALLUVION and DERELICTION.

Testamentary accretion. The accretion of LAPSED LEGACIES in favor of "the SUCCESSOR who, under the TESTAMENT, would have received the THING if the legacy had not been made." La. C.C. 1591. A legacy to a JOINT LEGATEE is divided among the other joint legatees. La. C.C. 1592. If the legatee is a child or sibling of the TESTATOR, his interest in the lapsed legacy goes to his descendants. La. C.C. 1593. The UNIVERSAL LEGATEE receives any lapsed legacies not otherwise disposed of. La. C.C. 1595.

Acknowledgment. A method of interrupting PRESCRIPTION in which a person recognizes "the right of the person against whom he had commenced to prescribe." La. C.C. art. 3464. For example, ACQUISITIVE PRESCRIPTION is interrupted when the party hoping to acquire the land acknowledges the ownership of the owner. Similarly, LIBERATIVE PRESCRIPTION is interrupted by a debtor acknowledging his debt. *Id.,* Comment (b). Acknowledgment can be formal, informal, written, oral, EXPRESS, or TACIT. *Id.,* Comments (c), (e). *See Flowers v. U.S. Fidelity & Guaranty Co.,* 381 So.2d 378 (La. 1979) (insurance company tacitly acknowledged a claim by making a partial payment).

Express Acknowledgment. A statement by which a person formally acknowledges the debt. Express acknowledgment can be made orally or in writing. *Flowers v. U.S. Fidelity & Guaranty Co.,* 381 So.2d 378, 382 (La. 1979), quoting BAUDRY-LACANTINERIE & TISSIER, 5 CIVIL LAW TRANSLATIONS, *Prescription* § 529, p. 261.

Tacit Acknowledgment. An ACKNOWLEDGMENT resulting

> from any action which amounts to an admission of the creditor's or owner's right, for instance the payment of a bill as debtor; payment of a portion of the debt, interests or arrears by the debtor or his agent; a request for a postponement of a payment; and, a fortiori, the payment of the amount due by the agent of the debtor. The same would be true of an offer to pay the damages caused by a tort, made

by the defendant in the course of the trial, or of an actual act of reparation or indemnity.

Flowers v. U.S. Fidelity & Guaranty Co., 381 So.2d 378, 382 (La. 1979), quoting AUBRY & RAU, 2 CIVIL LAW TRANSLATIONS *Property* § 215, No. 304, p. 344 (1966).

Acquets. Acquisitions. *See* La. C.C. 2327, Comment (b). The term is most often used in the phrase "community of acquets and gains," which refers to Louisiana's community property MATRIMONIAL REGIME. *See* La. C.C. art. 2326 *et seq.*

Acquisitive prescription. *See* PRESCRIPTION, ACQUISITIVE PRESCRIPTION.

Act. "Something done or performed, esp. voluntarily." BLACK'S LAW DICTIONARY, *act* (8th ed. 2004).

> **Act of administration.** A residual category of JURIDICAL ACT that includes "acts of management of a THING or of a PATRIMONY that exceed the limits of mere conservatory measures." YIANNOPOULOS, 3 LA. CIVIL LAW TREATISE § 87. *Contrast* ACT, CONSERVATORY ACT.

> **Act of disposition.** A JURIDICAL ACT that divests the owner of his interest in a THING or otherwise deprives him of some portion of a right in it. YIANNOPOULOS, 3 LA. CIVIL LAW TREATISE § 87.

> **Act under private signature.** A WRITING signed by the parties. *See* La. C.C. art. 1837.

> **Act translative of title.** A JURIDICAL ACT that, if executed by the true owner of a THING, would transfer ownership of that thing. *See* La. C.C. art. 3483, Comment (b). An act need not actually transfer ownership to be classified as an act translative of title. For example, a putative sale where the seller does not actually own the thing sold is an act translative of title.

> **Authentic act.**

> > A writing executed before a notary public ... in the presence of two witnesses, and signed by each party who executed it, by each witness, and by each notary

public before whom it was executed.

La. C.C. art. 1833.

Conservatory act. A JURIDICAL ACT aimed at protecting or preserving a THING within a PATRIMONY from damage, waste, or being lost. YIANNOPOULOS, 3 LA. CIVIL LAW TREATISE § 87.

Juridical act. A "manifestation of will intended to have legal consequences." La. C.C. art. 492, Comment (b).

Material act.

> [S]ome action or physical relationship to which the law attributes certain consequences. Such is the acquisition of the ownership of a thing by accession. Other material acts are the occupancy of a *res nullius*, the finding of a treasure or of lost things, and the writing of a literary work.

A.N. YIANNOPOULOS, CIVIL LAW SYSTEM: LOUISIANA AND COMPARATIVE LAW § 236, 447.

Preparatory acts. *Successions.* ACTS performed with or on succession property that do not imply acceptance of the succession, e.g., acts that could be classified as administrative, custodial, or preservative. La. C.C. art. 959.

Act of administration. *See* ACT, ACT OF ADMINISTRATION.

Act of disposition. *See* ACT, ACT OF DISPOSITION.

Act translative of title. *See* ACT, ACT TRANSLATIVE OF TITLE.

Act under private signature. A WRITING signed by the parties. *See* La. C.C. art. 1837.

Aleatory Contract. *See* CONTRACT, ALEATORY CONTRACT.

Alienation. The divestiture of the ownership of a THING.

Alimentary duties. The reciprocal OBLIGATIONS of descendants and ascendants to support one another. La. C.C. art. 229. The obligation includes the duty to provide the basic necessities of life—e.g., food, lodging, and healthcare—and, in the case of minors and certain adults, an education. *Id.* art. 230.

Alluvion. "ACCRETION formed successively and imperceptibly on the BANK of a river or stream, whether navigable or not." La. C.C. art. 499. The new land belongs to the owner of the bank on which the alluvion formed by ACCESSION.

Alluvion formed adjacent to properties owned by different people is divided equitably. La. C.C. art. 501. "When alluvion formed in front of the estates of riparian owners is to be divided, two objects, insofar as possible, are to be attained: (1) Each owner shall receive a fair proportion of the area of the alluvion, and (2) Each should receive a fair proportion of the new frontage on the water." *Jones v. Hogue*, 129 So.2d 194, 202 (La. 1960).

Alternative obligation. *See* OBLIGATION, ALTERNATIVE OBLIGA-TION.

Amicable compounder. An arbitrator "authorized to abate something of the strictness of the law in favor of natural equity." La. C.C. art. 3110.

Annuity. A contract "by which one party delivers to another a sum of money[] and agrees not to reclaim it so long as the receiver pays the rent agreed upon." La. C.C. art. 2793. The annuity may be for a stipulated term, perpetually, or for life. La. C.C. art. 2794. *See* YIANNOPOULOS, 2 LA. CIVIL LAW TREATISE § 150.

Antichresis. *See* PLEDGE, ANTICHRESIS.

Apparent servitude. *See* SERVITUDE, APPARENT SERVITUDE.

Appeal. An application to a higher court for the reversal of the decision of the lower court.

> **Devolutive appeal.** An appeal that does not suspend the effect or execution of the appealed judgment or order. *See* La. C.C.P. art. 2087.

> **Suspensive appeal.** An appeal that suspends the effect or execution of the appealed judgment during its pendency. *See*

La. C.C.P. art. 2123. Security must be furnished for a suspensive appeal. *Id.* art. 2124(B).

Arbitrator. A person who is not a judge but who is tasked with deciding a controversy between two or more persons. *Compare* AMICABLE COMPOUNDER.

Arpent. An area equaling approximately 0.85 acres. It can also refer to the length of the side of a square arpent, 191.83 feet.

Assigns. "Those to whom rights have been transmitted by particular title; such as sale, donation, legacy, transfer or cession." La. C.C. art. 3506(5).

Authentic act. *See* ACT, AUTHENTIC ACT.

Avulsion. The sudden tearing away of a piece of ground from one place along the BANK of a river or stream and subsequent attachment of that same ground to a bank downstream. The ownership of an identifiable piece of ground so carried away is not lost. La. C.C. art. 502.

B

Bank. The land adjacent to a navigable river, stream, or canal "lying between the ordinary low and the ordinary high stage of the water." La. C.C. art. 456. If there is a levee near the waterway, the bank lies between the water and the levee. *Id. See State v. Barras*, 602 So.2d 301 (La. App. 3 Cir. 1992) (A levee that is four or five miles away from the water is not near enough to the water to make the land between the water and that levee the bank.). *See, also,* BATTURE.

Batture. The land between a river and its levee. *See* BANK.

Bon père de famille. *French.* Literally, a "good father of the family." The phrase is better rendered as "good head of household." As used in the French Code Civil, it corresponds to the phrases "PRUDENT ADMINISTRATOR" and "prudent owner" found in Louisiana Law. La. C.C. art. 576, Comment (b). A bon père de famille is expected to exercise a heightened duty of diligence and care with regard to the maintenance and protection of those things entrusted to him in his capacity as administrator. *See id.*

Bornage. *French.* "The process of fixing and marking [a] BOUNDARY." La. C.C. art. 784, Comment (b). *See Lemoin v. Moncla*, 9 La.Ann. 515 (1854).

Boundary. "[T]he line of separation between contiguous lands." La. C.C. art. 784. The boundary is established either by an extra-judicial agreement or by the court according to TITLES, OWNERSHIP, or possession of the involved parties. La. C.C. arts. 789, 792–794. Any owner, USUFRUCTUARY, or LESSEE may compel a fixing of the subject land's boundaries. La. C.C. arts. 786, 787.

A boundary agreement is an ACT TRANSLATIVE OF TITLE; each party's ownership is modified to comport with the agreement. La. C.C. art. 795, Comment (b). If BOUNDARY MARKERS are mistakenly placed, the error may be corrected by a court, unless one of the owners has acquired ownership of the enclosed land by thirty-year ACQUISITIVE PRESCRIPTION. La. C.C. art. 796.

Boundary marker. "[A] natural or artificial object that marks on the ground the line of separation of contiguous lands." La. C.C. art. 784. For example, a fence might serve as an artificial boundary marker, or a stream might serve as a natural one.

Building restriction. "[C]harges imposed by the owner of an immovable in pursuance of a general plan governing building standards, specified uses, and improvements." La. C.C. art. 775. Generally, building restrictions are established in order to preserve the character or value of an area, subdivision, or the like. *See* YIANNOPOULOS, 4 LA. CIVIL LAW TREATISE § 191–200.

Building restrictions are established by JURIDICAL ACT and must be recorded to affect third persons. La. C.C. art. 776. Once established, building restrictions operate much like PREDIAL SERVITUDES, La. C.C. art. 777, but are actually *sui generis* REAL RIGHTS as long as the restrictions are part of a feasible general plan to which all covered properties are subject. La. C.C. art. 775, Comment (c); *Predial Servitudes* § 193.

Building restrictions may impose affirmative duties on the owners of subject estates, unlike predial servitudes. La. C.C. art.

778. However, the affirmative duties must be "reasonable and necessary for the maintenance of the general plan." *Id.*

Restrictions are most commonly enforced by injunctive relief. *See* La. C.C. art. 779. They may be altered or terminated in accordance with the act establishing them or by the rules set out in La. C.C. art. 780. The plan can also be abandoned tacitly or the situation of the land can change greatly enough to render the plan impossible. *See Robinson v. Donnell*, 374 So.2d 691 (La. App. 1 Cir. 1979) (restrictions abandoned when developer dug lake to be used for commercial purposes only on land originally restricted only to residential development).

In addition, a building restriction is extinguished by a violation that persists noticeably for two years. La. C.C. art. 780. After the extinction of the restriction, the land is treated as if it had never been subject to that restriction. *Id.*, Comment (b). Thus, building restrictions are subject to a two-year prescriptive period.

C

Caducity. The inheritable quality of a DONATION MORTIS CAUSA. *See* La. C.C. art. 880, Comment (b). "[T]he caducity or inheritable quality of a donation mortis causa can be destroyed or rendered ineffective ... by revocation by the TESTATOR [or] ... by lapse of the legacy." *Speller v. Herpel*, 357 So.2d 572, 574 (La. App. 1 Cir. 1978).

Caretaker. A "person legally obligated to provide or secure adequate care for a child, including a TUTOR, GUARDIAN, or legal custodian." La. C.C. art. 3469.

Cas fortuit. *French.* A fortuitous event. An OBLIGOR is freed from his OBLIGATION when his failure to perform is the result of a fortuitous event that renders the performance impossible, unless he has assumed the risk of that event. La. C.C. art. 1873. The term is interchangeable with "force majeure." *See id.*, Comment (c).

Cause. A reason why a party obligates himself. La. C.C. art. 1967. *See, generally, id.* arts. 1966–1970. A CONVENTIONAL OBLIGATION cannot exist without a lawful cause. La. C.C. arts. 1966–1967. An obligation can have many causes.

The reason why a party binds himself need not be to obtain something in return or to secure an advantage for himself. An obligor may bind himself by a gratuitous contract, that is, he may obligate himself for the benefit of the other party without obtaining any advantage in return.

Id. art. 1967, Comment (c); *id.* art. 1970, Comment (c).

Cause is not the same as common law consideration. For a discussion of the differences, *see* Christian Larroumet, *Detrimental Reliance and Promissory Estoppel as the Cause of Contracts in Louisiana and Comparative Law*, 60 TUL. L. REV. 1209 (1986).

> **Unlawful cause.** A CAUSE of an OBLIGATION which, if enforced, would "produce a result prohibited by law or against public policy." La. C.C. art. 1968.

Civil fruit. *See* FRUIT, CIVIL FRUIT.

Civil possession. *See* POSSESSION, CIVIL POSSESSION.

Clandestine possession. *See* POSSESSION, CLANDESTINE POSSESSION.

Collateral line. With respect to a person, a LINE of descendants who share a common ancestor with that person, e.g., uncles and cousins. La. C.C. art. 901.

Collateral mortgage. *See* MORTGAGE, COLLATERAL MORTGAGE.

Collateral relation. A member of the COLLATERAL LINE.

Collation. The actual or fictitious "return to the mass of the SUCCESSION which an HEIR makes of property which he received in advance of his share or otherwise, in order that such property may be divided together with the other effects of the succession." La. C.C. art. 1227. Goods are collated because it is presumed that the TESTATOR intended equality among his descendants. It follows, then, that anything the decedent gave to one of her future heirs before death constituted an advance on that heir's inheritance and that it should be taken into account in the distribution of the remainder decedent's estate. *See id.* art. 1229. Only the decedent's children who are forced heirs may demand collation, and only gifts made within three years of the decedent's death are subject to return. *Id.* art. 1235. For the rules of collation, *see, generally, id.* arts. 1227–1288.

Commodatum. The contract of LOAN FOR USE. *Contrast* MUTUUM.

Common thing. *See* THING, COMMON THING.

Commorientes. *Obsolete.* The phenomenon of several persons entitled to inherit from one another dying simultaneously in the same event (e.g., if a parent and child die simultaneously in an airplane crash), without any possibility of ascertaining who died first. The word "commorientes" is also used to refer to the decedents themselves. La. C.C. art. 936 (1870); Max Nathan, Jr., *Common Disasters and Common Sense in Louisiana*, 41 TUL. L. REV. 33, 40, n. 19 (1966). For an example, *see Blanchard v. Tinsman*, 445 So.2d 149 (La. App. 3 Cir. 1984), analyzing the consequences of a husband and wife dying as a result of a car crash.

Community of acquets and gains. The community property MATRIMONIAL REGIME of Louisiana under which spouses are CO-OWNERS of certain property that either spouse acquires during the marriage. La. C.C. arts. 2327, 2338–2340; *see, generally, id.* arts. 2334–2359.1.

Community property. Property belonging equally to both spouses under the community property MATRIMONIAL REGIME. *See* COMMUNITY OF ACQUETS AND GAINS.

Commutative Contract. *See* CONTRACT, COMMUTATIVE CONTRACT.

Compensation. An operation that takes place by law when two persons owe to each other sums of money or quantities of fungible THINGS identical in kind. Compensation reduces both obligations to the extent of the lesser amount. La. C.C. art. 1893. Compensation resembles common law set-off.

For example, if A owes B $1,000, and B owes A $500, the two obligations offset one another by $500; by operation of compensation A then owes B $500, and B owes A nothing.

Contractual compensation. *See* COMPENSATION, FACUL-TATIVE COMPENSATION.

Facultative compensation. COMPENSATION that takes place by virtue of an agreement between the parties to remove some obstacle that normally would prevent it—e.g., if the debt one party owes to the other is not liquidated or is subject to a term. La. C.C. art. 1901, Comment (a). Facultative compensation is also called CONTRACTUAL COMPENSATION.

Component part. A THING wholly incorporated into a tract of land or construction that ceases to have an independent existence and becomes an integral part of that IMMOVABLE. La. C.C. arts. 465–466.

Buildings or other constructions permanently attached to the ground, standing, timber, and unharvested crops or ungathered FRUITS of trees, are also component parts of a tract of land if they belong to the owner of the ground. La. C.C. art. 463. Component parts are similar to fixtures at common law.

Compromise. A "CONTRACT whereby the parties, through concessions made by one or more of them, settle a dispute or an uncertainty concerning an obligation or other legal relationship." La. C.C. art. 3071. A compromise is similar to the settlement of a lawsuit.

Concursus. A single proceeding in which multiple parties with conflicting claims to some asset or privilege litigate their claims. The person holding the asset delivers it to the court and is released from further liability for it to the claiming parties. The parties then must prove their claims to the asset. All parties are considered both plaintiffs and defendants. Like interpleader under the Federal Rules of Civil Procedure, concursus allows for a person with limited liability (e.g., an insurer who is responsible to several accident victims for the maximum amount of the insurance policy) to force the several claimants to litigate their claims in a single action, thereby limiting his exposure to duplicative damage awards that would exceed his liability. La. C.C.P. arts. 4651–4662.

Condition. "[A]n uncertain event upon which the enforceability of an obligation is made to depend." LITVINOFF, 5 LA. CIVIL LAW TREATISE § 5.3.

> **Potestative condition.** *Obsolete.* A condition that "makes the execution of the agreement depend on an event" that one of the parties may bring about or avoid. La. C.C. art. 2024 (1870). For a detailed discussion of potestative conditions and the jurisprudential considerations surrounding them, *see Long v. Foster & Associates, Inc.*, 129 So.2d 601 (La. App. 2 Cir. 1961) (holding that a clause in an employment contract allowing the employee to terminate his employment with two weeks' notice at any time constituted a potestative condition).

> **Resolutory condition.** A condition that, when fulfilled, terminates the obligation. La. C.C. art. 1767. For example, a lease contract that is conditioned on the lessee maintaining insurance on the premises terminates upon a lapse of insurance coverage. A resolutory condition is similar in some respects to the common law's condition subsequent.

> **Suspensive condition.** A condition that prevents an obligation from being enforced until it is fulfilled. La. C.C. art. 1767. For example, a construction contract conditioned upon a party supplying a construction bond is unenforceable until the bond is posted. A suspensive condition is similar in some respects to the common law's condition precedent.

> **Whimsical condition.** A SUSPENSIVE CONDITION that depends solely on the whim of the OBLIGOR.

Conditional obligation. *See* OBLIGATION, CONDITIONAL OBLIGATION.

Confusion. The extinction of an OBLIGATION when one person becomes both OBLIGOR and OBLIGEE. La. C.C. art. 1903. For example, a PREDIAL SERVITUDE is extinguished by confusion when the dominant and the servient estates are acquired in their entirety by one owner. *Id.* art. 765. Confusion is similar to the common law concepts of merger of rights, merger of title, and extinguishment.

Conjunctive obligation. *See* OBLIGATION, CONJUNCTIVE OBLIGATION.

Conservatory act. *See* ACT, CONSERVATORY ACT.

Consignment. The deposit of a THING or money with the court by the OBLIGOR after his OBLIGEE unjustifiably fails to accept delivery as required by the obligation. La. C.C. art. 1869. Consignation, if declared valid by a court, has the same effect as a performance under the obligation. *Id.*

Constructive possession. *See* POSSESSION, CONSTRUCTIVE POSSESSION.

Consumable. *See* THING, CONSUMABLE THING.

Contract. "[A]n agreement by two or more parties whereby obligations are created, modified, or extinguished." La. C.C. art. 1906. CONVENTIONAL OBLIGATIONS arise from contracts, although contracts are themselves sometimes erroneously referred to as conventional obligations. *See* La. C.C. arts. 1756–1757, 1906. *See, generally,* La. C.C. arts. 1906–2291 (Book III, Title IV, "Conventional Obligations or Contracts").

> **Accessory contract.** A CONTRACT made to depend on the existence and validity of another contract. Contracts for security, such as a MORTGAGE or PLEDGE, are accessory in nature and cannot exist independent of their principal contracts. *See* La. C.C. art. 1913.

> **Aleatory contract.** A CONTRACT in which the performance of either party's OBLIGATION or the extent of the performance depends on an uncertain event. La. C.C. arts. 1912, 2982–2984. *See, also,* CONDITION, SUSPENSIVE CONDITION. For example, a wager is an aleatory contract.

> **Bilateral contract.** A CONTRACT in which each party "obligates himself reciprocally, so that the OBLIGATION of each party is correlative to the obligation of the other." La. C.C. art. 1908. Many common contracts are bilateral. For example, the contract of SALE is a bilateral contract. Similar to a reciprocal contract at common law.

Commutative contract. A CONTRACT in which the performance of the OBLIGATION of each party is correlative to the performance of the other. A distinction is made between correlative obligations, which make a contract bilateral, and correlative performances, which make the contract not only bilateral but also commutative. *See* La. C.C. art. 1911, Comment (b). For example, the contract of SALE is commutative; the sale price given to the seller is correlative to the value of the THING sold. Otherwise, the sale may be rescinded for LESION.

Gratuitous contract. A CONTRACT in which the OBLIGOR obligates himself for the benefit of another without receiving any benefit in return. La. C.C. art. 1910. For example, many DONATIONS are gratuitous.

Innominate contract. CONTRACTS without a special designation or name. *Contrast* CONTRACT, NOMINATE CONTRACT.

Multilateral contract. A CONTRACT made by more than two parties. *See* La. C.C. art. 2020.

Nominate contract. A CONTRACT with a specific name, e.g., SALE, LEASE, LOAN, and insurance. La. C.C. art. 1914. *Contrast* CONTRACT, INNOMINATE CONTRACT.

Null contract. A CONTRACT for which the requirements of formation have not been met. La. C.C. art. 2029. E.g., a donation null in form.

Onerous contract. A CONTRACT in which "each of the parties obtains an advantage in exchange for his OBLIGATION." La. C.C. art. 1909. An exchange is the very essence of an onerous contract. *See* CAUSE. *See, also,* La. C.C. art. 1909, Comment (c).

Option contract. A CONTRACT "whereby parties agree that an offeror is bound by his offer for a specified period of time and that the offeree may accept within that time." La. C.C. art. 1933. An option contract differs from an IRREVOCABLE OFFER in that it "gives rise to rights and obligations that devolve upon the parties' heirs" and is assignable, *Id.*, Comment (b), whereas an irrevocable offer expires at the death of either party. La. C.C. art. 1932.

Principal contract. A CONTRACT that gives rise to the OBLIGATION for which an ACCESSORY CONTRACT is made to provide security. La. C.C. art. 1913. For example, if a person borrows money to purchase a house and gives a mortgage over the house to secure repayment, the loan contract is the principal contract to which the mortgage contract is accessory.

Synallagmatic contract. A BILATERAL CONTRACT.

Unilateral contract. A CONTRACT in which one party accepts the OBLIGATION of another but does not bind himself to perform a reciprocal obligation. La. C.C. art. 1907. For example, a DONATION is a unilateral contract.

The civilian conception of the unilateral contract differs from that of the common law. Under the common law, a unilateral contract is one in which one party makes a promise to perform and the other accepts with a performance. FARNSWORTH, CONTRACTS § 3.4 (4th ed.).

The Louisiana jurisprudence has occasionally confused the civilian meaning of the term with its common law cousin. For a broader exploration of the civilian unilateral contract, *see* Leonard Oppenheim, *The Unilateral Contract in the Civil Law and in Louisiana*, 16 TUL. L. REV. 456 (1942).

Contractual compensation. *See* COMPENSATION, FACULTATIVE COMPENSATION.

Conventional obligation. *See* OBLIGATION, CONVENTIONAL OBLIGATION.

Conventional servitude. *See* SERVITUDE, CONVENTIONAL SERVITUDE.

Co-owner. A person owning a thing together in indivision with one or more other people. *See* OWNERSHIP IN INDIVISION.

Corporeal. *See* THING, CORPOREAL THING.

Counterletter. In a SIMULATION, a counterletter is a writing separate from the simulated CONTRACT that describes the true intentions of the parties.

Curator. A person appointed by a court to care for the property or affairs of an absentee or an interdict. *See, e.g.*, La. C.C. arts. 47, 392. *See, also*, INTERDICTION.

Curatorship. *See* CURATOR; INTERDICTION.

Custom. A practice repeated for such a long time that it has been generally accepted as having the force of law. La. C.C. art. 3. "Custom may not abrogate legislation," *id.*, but it controls in the absence of legislation. La. C.C. art. 1. Courts may take notice of custom without it being raised by either party. YIANNOPOULOS, CIVIL LAW SYSTEM: LOUISIANA AND COMPARATIVE LAW § 92.

D

Damages.

> **Damages ex contractu.** Monetary damages awarded to an OBLIGEE for the OBLIGOR's failure or refusal to fulfill his OBLIGATION under a CONTRACT. *See* LITVINOFF, 6 LA. CIVIL LAW TREATISE § 3.1.

> **Damages ex delicto.** *See* DELICT.

> **Damages for nonpecuniary loss.** Damages recoverable for the breach of a CONTRACT intended to gratify a non-pecuniary interest when the OBLIGOR knew or should have known that his failure would cause such damage. La. C.C. art. 1998. For example, a buyer may recover damages for the disappointment he felt when his contract to purchase a horse he intended to exhibit was rescinded. *See Smith v. Andrepont*, 378 So.2d 479 (La. App. 1 Cir. 1979).
> "Regardless of the nature of the contract, these damages may be recovered also when the obligor intended, through his failure, to aggrieve the feelings of the OBLIGEE." La. C.C. art. 1998.

Dation en paiement. *French. See* GIVING IN PAYMENT.

Dative tutor. *See* TUTOR, DATIVE TUTOR.

De cujus. An old term for the decedent.

For example, "[i]n *Jackson v. United Gas Public Service Co.*, 196 La. 1, 198 So. 633 (1940), the issue was whether irregular heirs could sell an interest in property in a succession after the death of the de cujus but before judicial recognition of the heirs' interest." *West v. West*, 475 So.2d 56, 59 (La. App. 2 Cir. 1985).

Declinatory exception. *See* EXCEPTION, DECLINATORY EXCEPTION.

Degree. *Successions.* A generation. La. C.C. art. 900. For example, a father and son are separated by one degree.

Deimmobilization. The process by which COMPONENT PARTS of an IMMOVABLE are made distinct MOVABLES by an act translative of their ownership and delivery to acquirers in good faith or by their detachment and removal. La. C.C. art. 468.

For example, if the owner of a building decides to remove a brick façade and sells the bricks to a third party, those bricks cease to be component parts of the building and become distinct movables.

In addition, component parts of an immovable that are so damaged that they can no longer serve their function are deimmobilized by operation of law. *Id.* However, if the damaged things can be repaired, they remain immovables absent further action by the owner. *Folse v. Triche*, 113 La. 915, 920 (La. 1904).

See, generally, YIANNOPOULOS, 3 LA. CIVIL LAW TREATISE § 125.

Delict. *See* DÉLIT.

Délit. *French.* The civilian analog of tort.

> A tort is a civil wrong for which reparation is sought, normally in the form of an award of money damages. The word comes from the French word *tort*, or wrong, or from the Latin *tortus*, some conduct twisted from the norm. Formerly, the French used the term tort but now they have discarded it in favor of the word *délit* derived from the Latin term *delictum*.

BAILEY, 12 LA. CIVIL LAW TREATISE § 3.1.

The Louisiana Civil Code refers to delicts as offenses and quasi-offenses, which are the subject of articles 2315–2324. The articles are very broad and provide very little practical guidance.

The majority of Louisiana tort law has been created by the judiciary. *See id.* § 1.11.

Deposit. A CONTRACT whereby the depositor delivers a MOVABLE THING to the DEPOSITARY for safekeeping. The depositary is obliged to return the thing upon demand of the depositor. La. C.C. art. 2926. Deposit is very similar to bailment and can be either gratuitous or onerous.

The degree of care required of the depositary is dependent upon the nature of the contract. A compensated depositary must care for the deposit with diligence and prudence. La. C.C. art. 2930. But a gratuitous depositary must merely care for the deposit with the same diligence and prudence with which he cares for his own property. *Id.* Regardless of the nature of the deposit contract, a depositary who fails to meet the required standard of care is liable to his depositor for any loss the failure causes. *Id.*

> **Necessary deposit.** A deposit compelled by an accident, e.g., fire, the destruction of a house, shipwreck, or other casualty. La. C.C. art. 2964 (1870).

Depositary. The party with whom a DEPOSIT is placed.

Dereliction. Dry land revealed by water receding permanently and imperceptibly from the bank of a stream of river. La. C.C. art. 499. The new land is owned by owner of bank adjacent to the dereliction by ACCESSION.

Devolutive appeal. *See* APPEAL, DEVOLUTIVE APPEAL.

Dilatory exception. *See* EXCEPTION, DILATORY EXCEPTION.

Discussion. The "right of a secondary OBLIGOR to compel the creditor to enforce the OBLIGATION against the property of the primary obligor or, if the obligation is a legal or judicial MORT-GAGE, against other property affected thereby, before enforcing it against the property of the secondary obligor." La. C.C.P. art. 5151.

For example, if a person sues a partnership and its partners to enforce an obligation undertaken by the partnership, the partners may plead discussion of the partnership assets, which would require the plaintiff to exhaust all his rights against the property of the partnership before proceeding against the property of the individual partners. *See Koppers Co., Inc. v. Mackie Roofing and Sheet Metal Works*, 544 So.2d 25 (La. App. 4 Cir. 1989).

Disinherison. The deprivation by a TESTATOR of a FORCED HEIR of his LEGITIME. La. C.C. art. 1617. Disinherison must be made explicitly and for just cause in one of the manners prescribed for making a testament. La. C.C. arts. 1618–1619. Disinherison is similar to the common law's disinheritance.

There are only eight recognized reasons for disinherison: (1) the child has attempted to or has struck the parent; (2) the child commits cruel treatment, grievous injury, or a crime against the parent; (3) the child attempts to kill the parent; (4) the child unreasonably accuses the parent of a crime punishable by death or life imprisonment; (5) the child commits an act of violence or coercion to prevent the parent from making a testament; (6) the minor child marries without the parent's consent; (7) the child is convicted of a crime punishable by death or life imprisonment; and (8) the adult child who knows how to contact the parent fails to communicate with him for two years. La. C.C. art. 1621.

Disposable portion. Under the regime of FORCED HEIRSHIP, the portion of a decedent's estate not reserved for his FORCED HEIRS. La. C.C. art. 1495. *Viz.*, the disposable portion is the entire estate less the forced portion. *Contrast* LEGITIME. *See* FORCED HEIRSHIP.

Divisible obligation. *See* OBLIGATION, DIVISIBLE OBLIGATION.

Dol. *French.* FRAUD.

Domicile. The place where a person habitually resides. La. C.C. art. 38. Domicile requires both a physical presence in the parish of domicile and the intent to remain. *Becker v. Dean*, 854 So.2d 864, 871 (La. 2003).

A person may change his domicile by explicit declaration, *see* La. C.C. art. 45, or by tacit action, *see id.* art. 44. When the person has made no declaration of a change of domicile, there is a presumption against such a change. *Becker*, 854 So.2d at 871. In that case, his intention must be shown from the circumstances surrounding the controversy. La. C.C. art. 45.

Domicile is distinct from residency; a person always has exactly one domicile but can have many residences. *Id.* art. 39.

Dominant estate. The estate whose owner enjoys the rights created by a PREDIAL SERVITUDE. *Contrast* SERVIENT ESTATE.

Donation. A CONTRACT whereby a person called the donor irrevocably gives a THING to a person called the donee. Donation is often a GRATUITOUS CONTRACT.

> **Donation inter vivos.** A DONATION between living persons in which the donor irrevocably divests himself of a presently owned thing and the donee accepts it. La. C.C. art. 1468. There are three types of donation *inter vivos*: GRATUITOUS DONATIONS, ONEROUS DONATIONS, and REMUNERATIVE DONATIONS.

> **Donation mortis causa.** A DONATION that occurs upon the donor's death. Donations *mortis causa* may only be made by TESTAMENT.

> **Donation omnium bonorum.** A forbidden DONATION *inter vivos* in which a living person attempts to divest himself of his entire PATRIMONY without reserving to himself enough for his subsistence. La. C.C. art. 1498. A donation *omnium bonorum* is a nullity. *Id.*

> **Gratuitous donation.** An unconditional DONATION; a gift. *Contrast* ONEROUS DONATION; REMUNERATIVE DONATION.

> **Onerous donation.** A DONATION *inter vivos* in which the donee accepts the gift on condition that he fulfill a charge imposed on him by the donor. La. C.C. art. 1526. If the charges imposed outweighs the value of the thing donated, the transaction is not a donation. *Id.*
> Would-be heirs and legatees of a deceased donor have standing to challenge an onerous donation made during the donor's life if the donee subsequently fails to discharge his obligations. *See, e.g., Howard v. Administrators of Tulane Educational Fund*, 986 So.2d 47 (La. 2008).

> **Remunerative donation.** A DONATION given in repayment for services rendered. La. C.C. art. 1527. If the thing given is roughly equal in value to the services rendered, then the transaction is not a donation. *See* GIVING IN PAYMENT.

Duty-risk analysis. A test used by Louisiana courts to determine whether an alleged tortfeasor acted negligently. The test collapses the common law's duty and proximate cause into essentially one question: "[D]oes this defendant owe a duty to protect this plaintiff from this risk which occurred in this manner?" Thomas C. Galligan, Jr., *A Primer on the Patterns of Negligence*, 53 LA. L. REV. 1509, 1525 (1993).

See, also, Pitre v. Opelousas General Hosp., 530 So. 2d 1151, 1155 (La. 1988) (Parents sued doctor the doctor who performed a tubal ligation on the mother for failure to prevent their conceiving an albino child. The Court held that the doctor had a duty to inform the parents that the tubal ligation failed but that he had no duty to prevent the child's albinism.); and La. C.C. art. 2315 *et seq.*

E

Earnest money. A sum of money given by the buyer to the seller in connection with a contract to sell. Either party may recede from the contract. If the buyer does so, he forfeits the earnest money to the seller. On the other hand, if the seller recedes from the contract, he must return the earnest money to the buyer along with an equal sum. The parties must stipulate that the sum is earnest money and not a deposit on account of the price. La. C.C. art. 2624.

Emancipation. An ACT by which the effects of majority—e.g., the capacity to contract, personal liability for one's actions—are conferred on a minor. "There are three kinds of emancipation: JUDICIAL EMANCIPATION, EMANCIPATION BY MARRIAGE, and LIMITED EMANCIPATION BY AUTHENTIC ACT." La. C.C. art. 365.

> **Emancipation by ill treatment.** *Obsolete.* A "minor may be emancipated against the will of his [parents] when they ill treat him excessively, refuse him support, or give him corrupt examples." La. C.C. art. 368 (1870). *See, also,* La. C.C. art. 366, Comment (i).

> **Emancipation by marriage.** "A minor is fully emancipated by marriage." La. C.C. art. 367.

Emancipation conferring the power of administration. *Obsolete.* A minor who is fifteen years old or older may be emancipated by his father, mother, or both. The parents need only declare their intent to emancipate the child before a notary and two witnesses. La. C.C. art. 366 (1870). The emancipated minor then has the full administration of his estate. *Id.* art. 370 (1870).

The minor is not, however, cured of all of his contractual incapacity; he may only perform administrative acts, e.g., granting leases and receiving revenues. *Id.* Civil Code of 1870 articles 371 to 374 mark the boundaries of his power. For example, an emancipated minor can neither bind himself to pay a sum exceeding his gross income for one year, *Id.* art. 371 (1870), nor donate his property except by marriage contract and then only to his future spouse. *Id.* art. 374 (1870).

The emancipation can be revoked if the minor attempts contractually to exceed the limited capacity granted him by emancipation. *Id.* art. 377 (1870).

Judicial emancipation. A court may emancipate a minor who is sixteen years old or older for good cause. La. C.C. art. 366, La. C.C.P. art. 3991–3993. A judicial emancipation may be full or limited. La. C.C. art. 366. "Full judicial emancipation confers all effects of majority on the person emancipated, unless otherwise provided by law. Limited judicial emancipation confers the effects of majority specified in the judgment of limited emancipation, unless otherwise provided by law." *Id.*

Limited emancipation by authentic act. A minor's parents may emancipate him for the purpose of making certain specified JURIDICAL ACTS after he is sixteen years old. La. C.C. art. 368. This EMANCIPATION does not relieve them of liability for the damage he causes. *Id.*, Comment (a).

Emphyteusis. The CONTRACT of RENT OF LANDS.

Error. A mistake on the part of one of the parties to a CONTRACT. Error only vitiates a party's consent to the contract if it concerns the CAUSE of the OBLIGATION, the cause was known or should have been known to the other party, and the party in error would not have entered the agreement if he had known of his error. La. C.C. art. 1949.

> **Bilateral error.** A CONTRACT plagued by bilateral error may be rescinded or reformed to comport with the actual intent of the parties. *See* La. C.C. art. 1949, Comment (d).

> **Unilateral error.** A unilateral error can only vitiate the mistaken party's consent if the other party knew of or should have known the CAUSE for which the mistaken party made the agreement. *See* La. C.C. art. 1949, Comment (d).

Estate.

> **Dominant estate.** The land that enjoys the benefits of the charge placed on a SERVIENT ESTATE by a PREDIAL SERVITUDE.

> **Enclosed estate.** A parcel of land that has no access to a public road. *See* La. C.C. art. 689.

> **Estate of a deceased.** The "property, rights, and obligations that a person leaves after his death[, including] ... the rights and obligations as they exist at the time of death [and] all that ha[ve] accrued thereto since death and the new charges to which [the estate] becomes subject." La. C.C. art. 872. The estate is not a separate entity and has no personality. *Id.*, Comment.

> **Servient estate.** The land burdened by a PREDIAL SERVITUDE. *See* La. C.C. art. 646.

Estate debts. Debts of the decedent and administration expenses of his estate—e.g., burial expenses and maintenance fees for the decedent's property while it is under administration, respectively. La. C.C. art. 1415.

Étendue. *French.* Literally, "extent." In an ALEATORY CONTRACT, "the element of chance may rest in the extent (étendue), and not in the existence, of the obligation." La. C.C. art. 1912, Comment (f). For example, a party who agrees to support another for the rest of the latter's life has an OBLIGATION that comes into existence immediately, but the extent of the obligation depends on the length of the other party's life.

Eviction. A buyer's or lessor's loss of the thing sold or leased because of a third party's right that existed at the time of the SALE or LEASE. *See* La. C.C. arts. 2500, 2696. *See, also,* La. C.C. art. 3433, Comment (d).

Eviction can also refer to the action of a lessor to remove a lessee from the leased premises. *See* La. C.C.P. arts. 4701–4735.

Ex tunc. *Latin.* Literally, "from that time." An ex tunc effect is one that operates prospectively only. La. C.C. art. 2019, Comment (c).

Exception. A defendant's "means of defense ... to retard, dismiss, or defeat the demand brought against him." La. C.C.P. art. 921.

> **Declinatory exception.** An EXCEPTION in which the defendant urges the court to decline its jurisdiction without passing judgment on any substantive issues. La. C.C.P. art. 923. The defendant may urge in his declinatory exception, any of the following grounds or similar ones: insufficiency of citation or service of process, lis pendens, improper venue, and lack of personal or subject matter jurisdiction. La. C.C.P. art. 925.

> **Dilatory exception.** An EXCEPTION by which the defendant may retard the progress of the action without disposing of any substantive matters. La. C.C.P. art. 923. The dilatory exception may be grounded, for example, in the vagueness or ambiguity in the petition, the plaintiff's lack of procedural capacity, improper cumulation of actions, or improper joinder of parties. La. C.C.P. art. 926.

> **Peremptory exception.** An EXCEPTION in which the defendant seeks to have the action dismissed based on its legal nonexistence or its being barred by effect of law. La. C.C.P. art. 923. Peremptory exceptions may be raised because the claim has prescribed, the matter is res judicata, because there is no cause or right of action, or on similar grounds. La. C.C.P. art. 927.

Exchange. "[A] CONTRACT whereby each party transfers to the other the ownership of a THING other than money." La. C.C. art. 2660. The contract is also known as barter. *Contrast* SALE, in which the parties transfer the ownership a thing for money.

Executory proceeding. A proceeding used to cause the seizure and SALE of property to enforce a MORTGAGE or other PRIVILEGE without previous citation or judgment against the debtor. *See* La. C.C.P. art. 2631.

Executory process is often faster and cheaper than enforcing the privilege through an ordinary proceeding in which the creditor must first obtain a judgment against the mortgagor and then execute on the judgment. *See* La. C.C.P. art. 3722.

For a general discussion of mortgage enforcement using executory process, *see* Patrick S. Ottinger, *Enforcement of Real Mortgages by Executory Process*, 51 LA. L. REV. 87, 91 (1990).

Expense.

> **Expense for mere pleasure.** Expenses made only for the convenience or enjoyment of the owner or possessor of a THING that do not enhance the value of the thing. La. C.C. art. 1259. *Contrast* NECESSARY EXPENSE; USEFUL EXPENSE.

> **Necessary expense.** Indispensable expenses incurred for the preservation of a THING belonging to another or for the discharge of private or public burdens on the thing. La. C.C. art. 527, La. C.C. art. 1259. *Contrast* EXPENSE FOR MERE PLEASURE; USEFUL EXPENSE.

> **Useful expense.** Unnecessary expenses paid to enhance the value of land, e.g., the cost of raising a barn. La. C.C. art. 528, 1259. *Contrast* EXPENSE FOR MERE PLEASURE; NECESSARY EXPENSE.

Exposé des motifs. A report or explanation of the motives or reasons for passing a given statute.

Extraordinary repair. *See* REPAIR, EXTRAORDINARY REPAIR.

F

Facultative Compensation. *See* COMPENSATION, FACULTATIVE COMPENSATION.

Faculty. A patrimonial right not subject to LIBERATIVE PRESCRIP-TION, e.g., "the right of an owner to determine the mode of use of his immovable property and his rights to erect a building on a vacant lot, to demand the partition of property held in indivision, and to claim a forced passage in favor of an enclosed estate." 4 YIANNOPOULOS, LA. CIVIL LAW TREATISE § 196.

Falcidian portion. *Obsolete.* The one-fourth of the TESTATOR's estate that, under Roman law, had to be reserved to the INSTITUTED HEIR. The purpose of the falcidian portion was to protect the institutions of the family and its gods, rather than to benefit the testator's heirs directly. The falcidian portion was abolished in Louisiana.

Family. 1. In the most limited sense, father, mother, and children. 2. All the persons who live under the authority of another, including family servants. 3. All the relations descending from a common root. La. C.C. art. 3506(12).

Favor matrimonii. The policy of favoring the validity of a marriage when there is any reasonable basis to do so. La. C.C. 3520, Comment (b).

Favor testamenti. The policy of favoring the validity of a TESTAMENT when possible and when it is reasonably certain that the testament reflects the will of the TESTATOR. La. C.C. art. 3528, Comment (c).

Fideicommissa. *See* FIDEICOMMISSARY SUBSTITUTION.

Fideicommissary substitution. *See* SUBSTITUTION, VULGAR SUB-STITUTION.

Fidelity in marriage. The spouses' duty both to refrain from adultery and to submit to each other's reasonable sexual desires. La. C.C. art. 98, Comment (b).

First refusal, right of. A person's right to demand a seller offer to sell a thing to him before he offers to sell it to anyone else. La. C.C. art. 2625.

Fixing of the boundary. The action by which the BOUNDARY line between two adjacent pieces of land is, if uncertain or disputed, determined and, if markers were never placed, indicated by the placement of markers on the ground. La. C.C. art. 785. *See* YIANNOPOULOS, 2 LA. CIVIL LAW TREATISE § 282. The boundary may be fixed judicially or extrajudicially, i.e., by written agreement of the parties. La. C.C. art. 789.

The boundary is fixed judicially by a boundary action, which is a nominate REAL ACTION. *See* La. C.C.P. arts. 3691–3693. A landowner or one who possesses as owner has the right to bring the boundary action, La. C.C. art. 786, and that right is imprescriptible. *Id.* art. 788.

Force Majeure. Interchangeable with CAS FORTUIT.

Forced heirship. A legal regime in Louisiana in which certain descendants of the deceased, called forced heirs, are entitled to a certain portion of their ascendants' estates. This portion is called the LEGITIME, legal portion, FORCED PORTION, or legitimate portion. *See, generally,* La. C.C. arts. 1494–1514.

Forced portion. The portion of a decedent's estate that must be left to his forced heirs. *See* FORCED HEIRSHIP; LEGITIME.

Foreseeable. Falling "within the foresight of a reasonable man." La. C.C. art. 1996, Comment (b).

Fortuitous event. *See* CAS FORTUIT.

Fraud. A "misrepresentation or a suppression of the truth made with the intention either to obtain an unjust advantage for one party or to cause a loss or inconvenience to the other. Fraud may also result from silence or inaction." La. C.C. art. 1953.

Fraude. *French.* Literally, "cheating." The French distinguish between *dol*, "misrepresentation," and *fraude*. *Dol* is a misrepresentation meant to cause a person to enter into an agreement and corresponds to Louisiana's concept of fraud as defined in La. C.C. art. 1953. *Fraude*, on the other hand, is largely analogous to the American notion of expectation damages, *see* La. C.C. art. 1934 (1870); La. C.C. art. 1958.

Fruit. A THING "produced by or derived from another thing without diminution of [the latter's] substance. There are two kinds of fruits; natural fruits and civil fruits." La. C.C. art. 551.

> **Civil fruit.** "[R]evenues derived from a thing by operation of law or by reason of juridical act, such as rentals, interest, and certain corporate distributions." La. C.C. art. 551.

> **Natural fruit.** "[P]roducts of the earth or animals." La. C.C. art. 551.

Funeral charge. A charge incurred for the interment of the decedent. La. C.C. art. 3192.

Future thing, sale of. *See* SALE, SALE OF A FUTURE THING.

G

Garde. Custody or control over a thing. For example, in *Woods v. City of New Orleans*, City workers cut down an old bus sign, and someone tripped over the stub, injuring herself. The court found that the City "retained garde over the pole stub and concrete in which it was embedded" and, therefore, was liable for the plaintiff's injuries. 871 So.2d 1222, 1227 (La. App. 4 Cir. 2004).

General legacy. *See* LEGACY, GENERAL LEGACY.

General mortgage. *See* MORTGAGE, GENERAL MORTGAGE.

Giving in payment. An act whereby a debtor gives a THING to his creditor, who is willing to receive it, in payment of a sum which is due. The French phrase is *dation en paiement*. Similar to the common law concept of accord and satisfaction. *See* La. C.C. art. 2655.

Good faith. An important concept in several areas of the Civil Code. What exactly constitutes good faith depends on the behavior being examined. Good faith is described below in different contexts.

Accession. "For purposes of ACCESSION, a POSSESSOR is in good faith when he possesses by virtue of an ACT TRANSLATIVE OF OWNERSHIP and does not know of its defects." La. C.C. art. 487, Comment (b).

Acquisition of corporeal movable. "An acquirer of a CORPOREAL MOVABLE is in good faith ... unless he knows, or should have known, that the transferor was not the owner" of the transferred movable. La. C.C. art. 523.

Acquisitive prescription. "For purposes of ACQUISITIVE PRESCRIPTION, a POSSESSOR is in good faith when he reasonably believes, in light of objective considerations, that he is owner of the THING he possesses." La. C.C. art. 3480.

Marriage. Good faith exists where a putative spouse has "an honest and reasonable belief that there exists no legal impediment to [the] marriage." La. C.C. art. 96, Comment (d).

Gratuitous contract. *See* CONTRACT, GRATUITOUS CONTRACT.

Gratuitous donation. *See* DONATION, GRATUITOUS DONATION.

H

Habitation. *See* REAL RIGHT, HABITATION.

Hand note. *See* MORTGAGE, COLLATERAL MORTGAGE.

Heir. One who inherits from an INTESTATE SUCCESSION. La. C.C. arts. 876, 196. Such a person is also called an heir *ab intestato*.

Instituted heir. In a PROHIBITED SUBSTITUTION, the first donee who receives the property with the charge to preserve it and transmit it to the SUBSTITUTE HEIR upon the instituted heir's death. La. C.C. art. 1520. The instituted heir is often simply called the institute.

Substitute heir. In a PROHIBITED SUBSTITUTION, the second donee who receives the property upon the INSTITUTED

HEIR's death. La. C.C. art. 1520. The substitute heir is often simply called the substitute.

Unconditional heir. *Obsolete.* An heir who inherits "without any reservation, or without making an inventory." La. C.C. art. 882 (1870).

Heritable obligation. *See* OBLIGATION, HERITABLE OBLIGATION.

Héritage. *French.* Translated from the French language text of the Louisiana Civil Code as "estate," which was used to mean a distinct CORPOREAL IMMOVABLE. La. C.C. art. 646, Comment (b).

Homologation. Approval or confirmation. For example, if the HEIRS do not object to the TABLEAU OF DISTRIBUTION filed by the succession representatives, the court may homologate the tableau and order the representative to pay the debts listed thereon. *See* La. C.C.P. arts. 3303–3307. Similarly, if a CURATOR prays for the authority to sell the property of an interdict, the court may homologate and approve the application. *See id.* arts. 4271, 4566.

Hope, sale of a. An ALEATORY CONTRACT in which the seller sells the buyer an uncertain quantity of goods. La. C.C. art. 2451. For example, "a fisherman may sell the haul of his net before he throws it," *Id.*; a person may buy future crops and assume the entire risk of loss, *Losecco v. Gregory*, 32 So. 985 (La. 1901); or a buyer may purchase a house and assume the risk that he will be evicted soon after, *New Orleans & C.R. Co. v. Jourdain's Heirs*, 34 La.Ann. 648 (La. 1882). Unless the terms of the contract provide otherwise, the buyer assumes the risk that the hope will not materialize and he will receive nothing in return for the price paid.

Hors du commerce. *French.* Literally, "OUT OF COMMERCE."

Hypothecary action. An action instituted to enforce a MORTGAGE, sometimes called a CONTRACT of hypotheca (or hypothec), even if the property has been sold by the mortgagor to a third party. *See* PACT DE NON ALIENANDO.

I

Immovable. A tract of land and its COMPONENT PARTS, e.g., buildings and other permanent structures thereon. La. C.C. art. 462. This category of THINGS corresponds roughly to the common law's real property. *Contrast* MOVABLE.

> **Corporeal immovable**. An IMMOVABLE that can be touched and sensed, e.g., a tract of land. *Contrast* IMMOVABLE, INCORPOREAL IMMOVABLE.

> **Immovable by declaration.** Machinery, appliances, or equipment made into the COMPONENT PARTS of an IMMOVABLE onto which they are placed. In order to immobilize MOVABLES in this manner, the person must own the movables, own the immovable they are placed on, and file a declaration of immobilization in the public records. La. C.C. art. 467.

> **Immovable by destination.** *Obsolete.* "THINGS which the owner of a tract of land has placed upon it for its service and improvement are immovable by destination." La. C.C. art. 468 (1870). This category of things includes cattle intended for cultivation and related tools; seeds, plants, and fertilizer; beehives; pigeons and their coop; machinery to be used in plantation work; manufacturing equipment; refining and distilling equipment; and movables attached permanently to the building or land. *Id.*
>
> For a MOVABLE to become immovable by destination, it must have been used to serve or improve the agricultural or industrial uses of the land. *Straus v. City of New Orleans,* 118 So. 125, 130 (1928).
>
> In the 1978 revision of the Civil Code, the conceptual framework was simplified, and the classification of immovables by destination was abandoned. Some of the things that would previously have been considered immovables by destination may now be immobilized as component parts of the tract of land by a declaration of its owner. La. C.C. art. 467; YIANNOPOULOS, 2 LA. CIVIL LAW TREATISE § 113. *Compare* IMMOVABLE, IMMOVABLE BY DECLARATION.

Immovable by nature. *Obsolete.* "Wire screens, water pipes, gas pipes, sewerage pipes, heating pipes, radiators, electric wires, electric and gas lighting fixtures, bathtubs, lavatories, closets, sinks, gasplants, meters and electric light plants, heating plants and furnaces, when actually connected with or attached to the building by the owner for the use or convenience of the building are immovable by their nature." La. C.C. art. 467 (1870).

Article 467 of the Civil Code of 1870 was suppressed by the 1978 revision and replaced by the simplified conceptual framework for IMMOVABLE THINGS. *See* YIANNO-POULOS, 2 LA. CIVIL LAW TREATISE § 113. Things that were previously immovables by nature are now component parts of immovables. *See* La. C.C. art. 466. Neither the part's use for the convenience of the building nor the unity of ownership of the building and the part are required under the new definition. *Id.*, Comment (d).

Incorporeal immovable. "Rights and actions that apply to IMMOVABLE THINGS," including "PERSONAL SERVITUDES established on immovables, PREDIAL SERVITUDES, mineral rights, and PETITORY or POSSESSORY ACTIONS." La. C.C. art. 470. *Contrast* IMMOVABLE, CORPOREAL IMMOVABLE.

Implied Consent. "[A]ction or inaction that under the circumstances is clearly indicative of consent." La. C.C. art. 1927. Consent may be implied according to established custom and uses. La. C.C. art. 2457.

Impossibility of performance. A doctrine under which an OBLIGOR is relieved of his duty to perform by the occurrence of an event that renders that performance absolutely impossible. *See* La. C.C. art. 1873, Comment (d); *Eugster & Co. v. Joseph West & Co.*, 35 La.Ann. 119 (1883) (holding that the freezing of a river did not render the delivery of cargo impossible when the shipper could have shipped the goods before the freeze and other means of transport were available).

Improvement. A construction, planting, or work made on a tract of land. *See* La. C.C. arts. 496–497.

Inseparable improvement. An improvement to a tract of land that is "inseparable in [its] nature from the soil."

Gibson v. Hutchins & Vaughn, 12 La.Ann. 545, (1857). Drainage ditches, canals, and levees, for example, are inseparable immovables. La. C.C. art. 497, Comment (c); YIANNOPOULOS, 2 LA. CIVIL LAW TREATISE § 276.

Separable improvement. Improvements to a tract of land that may be separated from the land and removed. La. C.C. art. 497, Comment (c). This category of improvement includes houses, barns, carports, and other structures. *Id.*; YIANNOPOULOS, 2 LA. CIVIL LAW TREATISE § 276.

Imputation of payments. The express or tacit allocation of a payment to a certain debt by an OBLIGOR who owes several debts to one OBLIGEE, *viz.*, he imputes a particular payment to a particular debt. La. C.C. art. 1864.

In solido. *See* OBLIGATION, SOLIDARY OBLIGATION.

Incorporeal. *See* THING, INCORPOREAL THING.

Indivisibility. *Of mortgage.* The "notion that each portion of the mortgaged property secures every part of the mortgaged debt. ... Correlatively, each part of the obligation is secured by all of the mortgage over all of the property." La. C.C. art. 3280, Comment (a).

Indivisible obligation. *See* OBLIGATION, INDIVISIBLE OBLIGATION.

Indivision, ownership in. *See* OWNERSHIP, OWNERSHIP IN IN-DIVISION.

Ingratitude. *Donations.* A cause for the revocation of a DONATION *inter vivos.* La. C.C. art. 1556. Such a donation may only be revoked if "the donee has attempted to take the life of the donor;" or if "he has been guilty towards [the donor] of cruel treatment, crimes or grievous injuries." La. C.C. art. 1557.

Innkeeper. One who keeps "a tavern or hotel[] and make[s] a business of lodging travelers." La. C.C. art. 3232.

Innominate action. A legal action without a name prescribed by law, e.g., the REVENDICATORY ACTION.

Innominate contract. A CONTRACT without a special name. La. C.C. art. 1914. *Contrast* NOMINATE CONTRACT.

Insolvency. The state in which a person's liabilities exceed the value of his assets. La. C.C. art. 2037.

Inspection. *Sale.* The right of a buyer to inspect goods before or after delivery to ascertain their conformity to the terms of the CONTRACT. La. C.C. art. 2604.

Institute. *See* HEIR, INSTITUTED HEIR.

Instituted heir or legatee. *See* HEIR, INSTITUTED HEIR; FIDEICOMMISSA.

Intended use. *Sale.* Unless the seller knows of a particular use the buyer intends for the THING sold, a thing's ordinary use. La. C.C. art. 2475, Comment (b).

Inter vivos. *Latin.* Literally, "between living persons." *See* DONATION, DONATION INTER VIVOS.

Interdiction. The process by which an adult or an emancipated minor and his estate is placed under the care and control of a CURATOR. *See* La. C.C.P. arts. 4541–4556. A court may order the full interdiction of a person who, "due to an infirmity, is unable consistently to make reasoned decisions, and whose interests cannot be protected by less restrictive means." La. C.C. art. 389. Interdiction is similar to commitment in other states.

Interpretation. *Contracts.* The determination of the intent of the parties. La. C.C. art. 2045.

Interruption.

> **Interruption of possession.** *See* POSSESSION, INTERRUPTION OF POSSESSION.

> **Interruption of prescription.** *See* PRESCRIPTION, INTERRUPTION OF PRESCRIPTION.

Intestate. *Successions.* Without a TESTAMENT.

Intestate succession. The portion of a SUCCESSION in which the decedent's property devolves by operation of law instead of by testamentary bequest. La. C.C. arts. 875, 880. *See* La. C.C. Book III, Title I, Chapter 2.

Intestate successor. An HEIR *ab intestato* who inherits from an INTESTATE SUCCESSION.

Irresistible force. *See* CAS FORTUIT.

Irrevocable offer. *See* OFFER, IRREVOCABLE OFFER.

Item of performance. One of several parts of an OBLIGATION's PERFORMANCE. La. C.C. art. 1808, Comment (b). For example, an ALTERNATIVE OBLIGATION may bind the OBLIGOR to perform one of multiple items of performance—e.g., to give the OBLIGEE a painting or to pay him two hundred dollars, but not both.

J

Jactitation. *Obsolete.* A false claim repeated to the prejudice of another's right, similar to slander of title. The action to remedy this defamation or disturbance of title was known as the jactitatory action. In modern civil procedure, the jactitatory action has been replaced by the POSSESSORY ACTION.

Joint obligation. *See* OBLIGATION, JOINT OBLIGATION.

Juridical act. *See* ACT, JURIDICAL ACT.

Juridical person. *See* PERSON, JURIDICAL PERSON.

Jurisprudence constante. The doctrine under which a rule of law that has been accepted and applied repeatedly by the courts over a substantial period of time takes on great precedential weight for subsequent decisions. Jurisprudence constante is similar to stare decisis. "The most important differences between this civilian doctrine [of jurisprudence constante] and the common law rule of stare decisis may be summarized as follows: A single case affords sufficient foundation for the latter, while a series of adjudicated cases, all in accord, forms the basis for the former." A.N. YIANNOPOULOS, CIVIL LAW SYSTEM: LOUISIANA AND COMPARATIVE LAW § 97.

Just title. A "JURIDICAL ACT, such as a SALE, EXCHANGE, or DONATION, sufficient to transfer ownership or another REAL RIGHT. The act must be written, valid in form, and filed for registry in the conveyance records of the parish in which the IMMOVABLE is situated." La. C.C. 3483.

L

Lapsed legacy. *See* LEGACY, LAPSED LEGACY.

Last sickness. The sickness of which the debtor died. La. C.C. art. 3199.

Law.

Law charges. Charges incurred as a result of litigation, i.e., court costs. La. C.C. 3195. These debts enjoy a privilege over the debtor's MOVABLES second only to FUNERAL CHARGES. La. C.C. art. 3191.

Sources of law. LEGISLATION and CUSTOM. La. C.C. art. 1.

Lawful cause of preference. *See* PREFERENCE, LAWFUL CAUSES OF.

Lease. A "SYNALLAGMATIC CONTRACT by which one party, the LESSOR, binds himself to give to the other party, the LESSEE, the use and enjoyment of a THING for a TERM in exchange for a RENT that the lessee binds himself to pay." La. C.C. art. 2668.

Lease of labor or industry. A NOMINATE CONTRACT whereby a person agrees to perform certain services for a price. *See* La. C.C. art. 2745. The lease creates an employer-employee relationship between the parties. *Hughes v. Goodreau*, 836 So.2d 649, 655 (La. App. 1 Cir. 2002).

Legacy. A DONATION MORTIS CAUSA made by TESTAMENT.

> **General legacy.** A LEGACY by which the TESTATOR bequeaths a fraction of his estate or the remainder of the balance of the estate after PARTICULAR LEGACIES are taken out. La. C.C. art. 1586.
>
> **Joint legacy.** A LEGACY made to several LEGATEES without the assignment of shares to each legatee. La. C.C. art. 1588.
>
> **Lapsed legacy.** A LEGACY that is no longer valid for one or more of the following reasons: "the LEGATEE predeceases the TESTATOR[;] the legatee is incapable of receiving at the death of the testator[;] the legacy is subject to a SUSPENSIVE CONDITION, and the condition can no longer be fulfilled or the legatee dies before [fulfilling] the condition[;] the legatee is declared UNWORTHY[;] the legacy is renounced, but [the legacy lapses] only to the extent of the renunciation[;] the legacy is declared invalid[; or] the legacy is declared NULL." La. C.C. art. 1589.
>
> **Legacy under particular title.** The testamentary disposition of a certain object. Legacies under particular title form the residual category of legacies. La. C.C. art. 1587.
>
> **Legacy under universal title.** *Obsolete.* A GENERAL LEGACY. La. C.C. art. 1586, Comment (a).
>
> **Particular legacy.** *See* LEGACY, LEGACY UNDER PARTICULAR TITLE.
>
> **Separate legacy.** A LEGACY made to several LEGATEES who are each assigned a share by the TESTATOR. La. C.C. art. 1588.
>
> **Universal legacy.** A LEGACY "of all the estate, or the balance of the estate that remains after PARTICULAR LEGACIES" made for the benefit of one or more LEGATEES. La. C.C. art. 1585.

Legal servitude. *See* SERVITUDE, LEGAL SERVITUDE.

Legal usufruct. *See* USUFRUCT, LEGAL USUFRUCT.

Legatee. A testate successor. La. C.C. art. 876. *See* SUCCESSION, TESTATE SUCCESSION.

Legislation. A "solemn expression of legislative will." La. C.C. art. 2.

Legitimation. The process by which an illegitimate child is made legitimate, e.g., by the subsequent marriage of their father and mother, whenever the parents have formally or informally acknowledged them as their children, either before or after the marriage.

Legitime. The portion of a decedent's estate reserved to the FORCED HEIR. La. C.C. art. 1494. *Contrast* DISPOSABLE PORTION. *See* FORCED HEIRSHIP; DISINHERISON; MARITAL PORTION.

Lesion. *French.* Literally, "injury."

> **Lesion among co-owners.** The source of a former co-owner's right to rescind an extrajudicial PARTITION if the value he received for his portion of the partitioned property was less than three-quarters of the fair market value of the property. La. C.C. art. 814.

> **Lesion beyond moiety.** The source of a seller's right to rescind the SALE of a CORPOREAL IMMOVABLE when he received a price less than half the fair market value of the THING. La. C.C. art. 2589. A party may also rescind the transaction when he exchanges an immovable for MOVABLES worth less than half the fair market value of the immovable. La. C.C. art. 2663.

Lessee. The party to a LEASE who binds himself to pay the RENT. La. C.C. art. 2668.

Lessor. The party to a LEASE who binds himself to give the LESSEE the use or enjoyment of the leased THING. La. C.C. art. 2668.

Lessor's privilege. The PRIVILEGE that a LESSOR enjoys over MOVABLES found in or upon the leased property belonging to the LESSEE to secure the payment of RENT or the performance of any other OBLIGATION related to the lease. La. C.C. art. 2707.

Lex causae. *Latin, plural* leges causae. Literally, "law of the case." The "substantive law which, through the choice-of-law rules of the forum, is found applicable to the merits of a particular action that contains foreign elements." La. C.C. art. 3549, Comment (b).

Lex fori. *Latin.* Literally, the "law of the forum." The "law of the state where litigation takes place." La. C.C. art. 3549, Comment (b).

Liability in solido. *See* SOLIDARY LIABILITY.

Liberative prescription. *See* PRESCRIPTION, LIBERATIVE PRE-SCRIPTION.

Line. *Successions.* A series of DEGREES from one person to his relatives through his family tree. La. C.C. art. 901. For example, the chain from grandmother to mother to child forms a line.

> **Collateral line.** "[T]he series of DEGREES between persons who do not descend from one another, but who descend from a common ancestor," as do, e.g., siblings or cousins. La. C.C. art. 901. The number of degrees in the collateral line is calculated by counting the number of generations between the HEIR and common ancestor and adding the number of generations between the decedent and the common ancestor. *Id.* For example, there are two degrees in the collateral line between siblings.

> **Direct line.** "[T]he series of DEGREES between persons who descend from one another." La. C.C. art. 901. The number of degrees in the direct line is the number of generations between the HEIR and the decedent. *Id.* For example, a grandchild and his grandparent are separated by two degrees.

Litigious right. A right that is contested in a suit already filed. La. C.C. 2652. *See* SALE, SALE OF A LITIGIOUS RIGHT.

Loan.

> **Loan for consumption.** A "CONTRACT by which a person, the lender, delivers CONSUMABLE THINGS to another, the borrower, who binds himself to return to the lender an equal

amount of things of the same kind and quality." La. C.C. art. 2904. The contract is also known as MUTUUM. *Contrast* LOAN, LOAN FOR USE; COMMODATUM.

Loan for use. A GRATUITOUS CONTRACT "by which a person, the lender, delivers a NONCONSUMABLE THING to another, the borrower, for him to use and return." La. C.C. art. 2891. The contract is also known as COMMODATUM. *Contrast* LOAN, LOAN FOR CONSUMPTION; MUTUUM.

Lost thing. *See* THING, LOST THING.

Lump sale. *See* SALE, LUMP SALE.

M

Management of affairs. A non-contractual relationship that arises from "a person, the manager, [acting] without authority to protect the interests of another, the owner, in the reasonable belief that the owner would approve of the action if made aware of the circumstances." La. C.C. art. 2292. The manager is bound to act as a prudent administrator, La. C.C. art. 2295, and the owner is bound to honor the OBLIGATIONS undertaken by the manager and to reimburse him for all NECESSARY and USEFUL EXPENSES. La. C.C. art. 2297. Also called NEGOTIORUM GESTIO.

Mandatary. A person empowered by a MANDATE to act for another and in his name. Similar to an agent at common law. *See* MANDATE.

Mandate. "[A]n ACT by which one person, the principal, confers authority on another person, known as the MANDATARY, to transact one or more affairs for the principal" in his name. La. C.C. art. 2989. Synonymous with contractual agency.

Mandatory law. A class of provisions from which parties may not derogate in crafting agreements. For example, rules of public order are mandatory laws. *See* La. C.C. art. 2802, Comment (b). *Contrast* SUPPLETIVE LAW.

Manual gift. The DONATION of a CORPOREAL MOVABLE accompanied by actual delivery. La. C.C. art. 1543. This species of donation is not subject to any formal requirements. *Id.*

Marital portion. A portion of a decedent's estate to which his surviving spouse is entitled if he dies rich in comparison to her. La. C.C. art. 2432. The portion is limited to one million dollars. La. C.C. art. 2434.

It is determined by the number of children left by the decedent. If he dies without children, the portion is one quarter of his succession in full ownership. *Id.* If he dies with one to three children, the portion is a lifetime USUFRUCT over one quarter of the estate. *Id.* Finally, if he leaves four or more children, the portion is equal to a lifetime usufruct over one child's share. *Id.* Any LEGACY left to the surviving spouse is deducted from the marital portion to which she would be entitled.

Marriage. A "legal relationship between a man and a woman that is created by civil contract." La. C.C. art. 86.

> **Absolutely null marriage.** A MARRIAGE "contracted without a marriage ceremony, by procuration [i.e., on behalf of one or both of the parties by a representative], or in violation of an impediment [e.g., consanguinity or bigamy]." La. C.C. 94. Such a marriage "nevertheless produces civil effects in favor of a party who contracted it in good faith for as long as that party remains in good faith" and in favor of the children of that marriage. La. C.C. art. 96. *See* La. C.C. arts. 90, 92.

> **Marriage contract.** A MATRIMONIAL AGREEMENT.

> **Putative marriage.** An absolutely null MARRIAGE that produces civil effects. *See* La. C.C. art. 96.

> **Relatively null marriage.** A MARRIAGE in which the consent of one of the parties was not freely given. La. C.C. art. 95. "Such a marriage may be declared null upon application of the party whose consent was not free[ly given]." *Id.* But that party may also ratify the marriage after overcoming his incapacity. *Id.*

Masters of boarding houses. "[A]ll persons who make a business of receiving persons at board for a fixed price." La. C.C. art. 3211.

Material act. *See* ACT, MATERIAL ACT.

Material alteration. *Contracts.* An alteration to the terms of an agreement by the acceptance of an OFFER that "gives rise the presumption that the offeror would not enter a CONTRACT with that term." La. C.C. art. 2601, Comment (g). *See* La. C.C. arts. 2601 (alterations of the terms of a sale) and 1943 (general treatment of an acceptance with terms that vary from the offer).

Matrimonial agreement. A "CONTRACT establishing a regime of SEPARATION OF PROPERTY [as opposed to COMMUNITY PROPERTY] or modifying or terminating that regime." La. C.C. art. 2328. Under the Civil Code of 1870, a matrimonial agreement was a species of marriage contract, i.e., an antenuptial agreement. *Id.*, Comment (c). Under the current revision, the two terms—marriage contract and matrimonial agreement—have the same meaning, but a matrimonial agreement can be executed both before or during a marriage. *Id.*

Matrimonial regime. A "system of principles and rules governing the ownership and management of the property of married persons as between themselves and toward third persons." La. C.C. art. 2325. *See* COMMUNITY PROPERTY.

Mineral. A naturally occurring PRODUCT like oil, gas, or coal. *See* Louisiana Mineral Code, La. R.S. Title 31.

Monition. An advertisement made in a newspaper advertising property purchased at a sheriff's or judicial SALE and calling for any person having an interest in that property or knowing of any irregularity in the procedure of its sale to show why the purchaser's rights in the property should not be confirmed. *See, generally*, La. R.S. 13:4941–4950.

Moral damages. Damages for non-pecuniary loss, e.g., mental anguish.

Moratory damages. Damages for a delay in the performance of an OBLIGATION. La. C.C. art. 1989; *id.*, Comments (a), (b).

Mortgage. A "nonpossessory right created over property to secure the performance of an OBLIGATION." La. C.C. art. 3278. "Mortgage gives the MORTGAGEE, upon failure of the OBLIGOR to perform the obligation that the mortgage secures, the right to cause the property to be seized and sold ... and to have the proceeds applied toward the satisfaction of the obligation in preference to claims of others." *Id.* art. 3279.

> **Collateral mortgage.** A hybrid security device created by Louisiana's practitioners in which a borrower executes a promissory note payable to the bearer and secured by a MORTGAGE. A notary PARAPHS the promissory note to identify it as being secured by the mortgage. Then, the mortgagor PLEDGES the mortgage package—the paraphed note and act of mortgage—to secure a second promissory note, called the HAND NOTE, which represents the actual debt. For a thorough discussion of collateral mortgages and how they differ from conventional mortgages, *see* Max Nathan, Jr. & H. Gayle Marshall, *The Collateral Mortgage*, 33 LA. L. REV. 497 (1973).

> **Conventional mortgage.** A MORTGAGE established by CONTRACT. La. C.C. art. 3284.

> **General mortgage.** A MORTGAGE over all the present and future property of the OBLIGOR. La. C.C. art. 3285.

> **Judicial mortgage.** A MORTGAGE "established by law to secure a judgment" for the payment of money. La. C.C. arts. 3284, 3299.

> **Legal mortgage.** A MORTGAGE "established by operation of law" securing "an OBLIGATION specified by the law that provides for the mortgage." La. C.C. art. 3284, 3299. For example, a TUTOR's obligation toward a minor is secured by a legal mortgage over the tutor's property. La. C.C. art. 322.

> **Special mortgage.** A MORTGAGE over specific property of the MORTGAGOR. La. C.C. art. 3285. For example, the CONVENTIONAL MORTGAGE used to finance a house is often a special mortgage over that house alone (as opposed to over

all of the mortgagor's property). *Contrast* MORTGAGE, GEN-ERAL MORTGAGE.

Mortgagee. The "creditor or creditors to whom OBLIGATIONS are owed that from time to time are secured by the MORTGAGE." La. C.C. art. 3279, Comment (a).

Mortgagor. The debtor who mortgages his property to secure an OBLIGATION he owes.

Mortis causa. *Latin.* Literally, "on the occasion of death." *See, e.g.,* La. C.C. art. 1469; DONATION, DONATION MORTIS CAUSA.

Movable. The residual category of THINGS: any thing—corporeal or incorporeal—that is not classified as an IMMOVABLE is a movable. La. C.C. art. 475. Similar to the common law's personalty or chattels.

> **Corporeal movable.** An animate or inanimate THING that normally moves "or can be moved from one place to another." La. C.C. art. 471.

> **Incorporeal movable.** "Rights, OBLIGATIONS, and actions that apply to a movable thing," e.g., "bonds, annuities, and interests or shares in entities possessing juridical personality." La. C.C. art. 473.

Mutuum. A LOAN FOR CONSUMPTION.

Mystic testament. *Obsolete. See* TESTAMENT, MYSTIC TESTAMENT.

N

Naked owner. The person holding the NAKED OWNERSHIP of a thing.

Naked ownership. "The ownership of a thing burdened with a USUFRUCT." La. C.C. art. 478. Similar to the residue of a life estate at common law.

Natural fruit. *See* FRUIT, NATURAL FRUIT.

Natural obligation. *See* OBLIGATION, NATURAL OBLIGATION.

Natural person. *See* PERSON, NATURAL PERSON.

Natural servitude. *See* SERVITUDE, NATURAL SERVITUDE.

Navigable body of water. A body of water "susceptible of being used, in its ordinary condition, as a highway of commerce over which trade and travel are or may be conducted in the customary modes of trade and travel on water." YIANNOPOULOS, 2 LA. CIVIL LAW TREATISE § 64.

Ne varietur. *Latin.* Literally, "it must not be altered." The phrase is usually found as part of a PARAPH.

Negotiorum gestio. *Latin.* Literally, "management of another's affairs." *See* MANAGEMENT OF AFFAIRS. *Contrast* MANDATARY.

Negotiorum gestor. The benevolent party who intervenes in the affairs of another in the absentee's absence. *See* NEGOTIORUM GESTIO.

Nominate action. A legal action with a name prescribed by law, e.g., POSSESSORY ACTION.

Nominate contract. *See* CONTRACT, NOMINATE CONTRACT.

Non-alienation pact. *See* PACT DE NON ALIENANDO.

Nonapparent servitude. *See* SERVITUDE, NONAPPARENT SERVITUDE.

Nonconsumable. *See* THING, NONCONSUMABLE THING.

Novation. The "extinguishment of an existing OBLIGATION by the substitution of a new one." La. C.C. art. 1879.

> **Objective novation.** An agreement substituting a new performance or CAUSE for the performance required by or the cause underlying the original OBLIGATION. La. C.C. art.

1881. For example, a creditor may agree to have his debtor discharge the debt by giving him a thing instead of paying money, as had previously been agreed; since a different performance is now required, an objective novation has taken place.

But if a substantial part of the obligation is still required, the agreement is not a novation. *Id.* Regardless, the parties may effect a novation by declaring their intention to novate the obligation, even though they do not substitute a new performance or cause. *Id.*; and *id.*, Comment (d).

Subjective novation. A NOVATION by which the OBLIGEE substitutes a new OBLIGOR for the previous one. The previous obligor is thereby discharged from his OBLIGATION. La. C.C. art. 1882. The former obligor's consent is not required unless he had an interest in performing the obligation himself. *Id.*

Nulla bona. *Latin.* Literally, "no goods." A return from a writ of fieri facias that indicates that the debtor has no property that can be seized. *See, e.g., Wheeling Pottery Co. v. Levi,* 19 So. 752, 753 (La. 1896) ("The return of the writ nulla bona is evidence of the debtor's insolvency, or that he has no property within the court's process.").

Nullity. A JURIDICAL ACT deprived of its normal effects by the law for reasons that have existed since the inception of the act. SAÚL LITVINOFF & W. THOMAS TÊTE, LOUISIANA LEGAL TRANSACTIONS: THE CIVIL LAW OF JURIDICAL ACTS 162 (1969).

Absolute nullity. A JURIDICAL ACT that violates a rule of public order. *See* La. C.C. art. 2030. An absolute nullity is without any effect whatsoever, and the nullity of the act may be invoked by any person or by the court *sua sponte. Id.* For example, a bigamous MARRIAGE is an absolute nullity.

Relative nullity. A JURIDICAL ACT that violates a rule intended for the protection of a private party. *See* La. C.C. art. 2031. A relative nullity may be confirmed only by the party whose interests are protected by the rule being violated. *Id.* For example, a CONTRACT that is relatively null because of a VICE OF CONSENT may be confirmed after the vice is removed. Similarly, only the protected party may invoke the act's nullity to avoid its effects. *Id.*

Nuncupative testament. *Obsolete. See* TESTAMENT, NUNCUPATIVE TESTAMENT.

O

Objective novation. *See* NOVATION, OBJECTIVE NOVATION.

Obligation. A "legal relationship whereby a person, called the OBLIGOR, is bound to render a performance in favor of another, called the OBLIGEE," that consists of giving, doing, or not doing something. La. C.C. art. 1756.

> **Accessory obligation.** An OBLIGATION that depends on the existence of another obligation for its own existence. For example, an obligation to provide security for another obligation is accessory and ceases to exist when the principal obligation is performed. *Compare* CONTRACT, ACCESSORY CONTRACT.

> **Alternative obligation.** An OBLIGATION in which the OBLIGOR is bound to render exactly one of several possible items of performance. La. C.C. art. 1808.

> **Civil obligation.** *Obsolete.* A "legal tie, which gives the party[] with whom it is contracted[] the right of enforcing its performance by law." La. C.C. art. 1757 (1870). *Contrast* OBLIGATION, NATURAL OBLIGATION and IMPERFECT OBLIGATION.

> **Community obligation.** "An OBLIGATION incurred by a spouse during the existence of a COMMUNITY PROPERTY REGIME for the" interest of the other spouse or of both spouses together. La. C.C. art. 2360. For example, a loan to purchase a family home would create a community obligation.

Conditional obligation. An OBLIGATION which depends upon the occurrence or nonoccurrence of an uncertain event. La. C.C. art. 1767. *See* CONDITION.

Conjunctive obligation. An OBLIGATION that "binds the OBLIGOR to multiple items of performance that may be separately rendered or enforced." La. C.C. art. 1807. The parties, by agreement, may provide that the obligor's failure to render any one of the items of performance will allow the OBLIGEE to demand the remainder of the performance immediately, i.e., acceleration. *Id.* For example, a LEASE which calls for rent payments to be made monthly creates a conjunctive obligation.

Conventional obligation. An OBLIGATION created by a CONTRACT.

Divisible obligation. An OBLIGATION in which the object of the performance is, by its nature, divisible. La. C.C. 1815. For example, an obligation to pay money is inherently divisible.

Heritable obligation. An OBLIGATION in which the requirement of performance may be transferred to another or which may be enforced by a successor of the OBLIGOR. La. C.C. art. 1765. All obligations are heritable, unless the parties agree or the nature of the performance dictates otherwise. *Id. Contrast* OBLIGATION, STRICTLY PERSONAL OBLIGATION.

Imperfect obligation. *Obsolete.* An OBLIGATION that creates a moral duty to perform but does not give the OBLIGEE any enforceable right or any cause of action. La. C.C. art. 1757(1) (1870). The category was eliminated by revision because it has no legal effect. La. C.C. art. 1760, Comment (d). *Contrast* OBLIGATION, NATURAL OBLIGATION.

Indivisible obligation. An OBLIGATION in which "the object of the performance ... is not susceptible of division." La. C.C. art. 1815. "[S]ome things that may be the objects of performance are ... indivisible because of their nature, as in the case of a live animal or a painting." LITVINOFF, 5 LA. CIVIL LAW TREATISE § 9.3.

Other things are relatively indivisible "when different, separable parts of a thing constitute a harmonious whole, as in the preferred example of a building that, though constructed in stages and by workmen of different trades, will not satisfy the interest of the OBLIGEE, or owner, unless it is completed." *Id.*

The parties to the contract giving rise to the obligation may agree to treat the object of the performance as if it were indivisible, thus creating a conventionally indivisible object. *Id.* § 9.5; La. C.C. art. 1815.

Joint obligation. With respect to the OBLIGORS, an OBLIGATION is joint when many obligors owe a single performance to one OBLIGEE but no obligor is liable for the entire performance. La. C.C. art. 1788. For example, a partnership is liable for its debts, but if it cannot pay those debts, the each partner is individually liable for his VIRILE SHARE of the debts. The partners, then, are jointly liable for the payment of the partnership's debts.

With respect to the obligees, an obligation is joint when a single obligor owes a performance to many obligees but no obligee is entitled to the whole performance. *Id.* For example, if several landowners execute a single mineral lease on the condition that the lessee will drill within a certain time, that lease is joint with respect to the landowners. If the lessee drills on land owned by one of them but not on the others' land, the condition is satisfied. *See Nabors v. Producers' Oil Co.*, 74 So. 527 (La. 1917).

Natural obligation. An OBLIGATION arising "from circumstances in which the law implies a particular moral duty to render a performance." La. C.C. art. 1760. It may not be enforced by judicial action, but whatever performance has been freely made in satisfaction of the natural obligation may not be reclaimed. *Id.* art. 1761. *See* REPETITION. "A CONTRACT made for the performance of a natural obligation is onerous." *Id.*

For example, a natural obligation to pay remains after a debt is extinguished by LIBERATIVE PRESCRIPTION. *See* La. C.C. art. 3447, Comment (b). The concept of natural obligations is similar to that of moral consideration in the common law.

Principal obligation. An OBLIGATION upon which an ACCESSORY OBLIGATION depends for its existence. For example, where the performance of one obligation is secured by another, the former is the principal obligation.

Real obligation. A "duty correlative to and incidental to a REAL RIGHT." La. C.C. art. 1763. "An example of a real obligation is the duty imposed by Article 746 of the Civil Code on the owner of a SERVIENT ESTATE to construct at his expense works necessary for the exercise of a servitude." YIANNOPOULOS, 2 LA. CIVIL LAW TREATISE § 203.

Separate obligation. *Community property.* An OBLIGATION incurred by a spouse prior to the establishment of a COMMUNITY PROPERTY REGIME; during the regime but not for the common interest of the spouses or of the other spouse; after the termination of the community; or "for the separate property of a spouse to the extent that it does not benefit the community, the family, or the other spouse." La. C.C. art. 2363. Alternatively, an obligation "resulting from an intentional wrong" that does not benefit the community, the other spouse, or the family. *Id.*

Several obligation. An OBLIGATION in which there are multiple parties on the one hand—either as OBLIGEES or OBLIGORS—and a single party on the other. La. C.C. art. 1787.

An obligation in which each of several obligors owes an individual performance to one obligee is several with respect to the obligors. *Id.* For example, if one obligor gives the obligee money and another must give a THING, the obligation is several with respect to the obligors. *See id.,* Comment (b).

An obligation in which a single obligor owes a discrete performance to each of a number of obligees is several with respect to the obligees. *Id.* For example, an obligor's obligation to make payments to the plaintiffs in a successful class action suit is several with respect to the obligees.

Solidary obligation. An OBLIGATION in which the entire performance owed may be demanded of a single OBLIGOR or by a single OBLIGEE. La. C.C. art. 1790, 1794. An obligation is solidary with respect to the obligees if one of a set of obligees may demand the entire performance from their common obligor. *Id.* art. 1790. Conversely, an obligation is solidary with respect to the obligors if each obligor is liable for the whole performance. *Id.* art. 1794. In that case, one obligor's performance relieves the rest of liability to the obligee. *Id.* For example, conspirators who commit an intentional tort are solidarily liable for the harm they cause. La. C.C. art. 2324. *See* SOLIDARY LIABILITY; VIRILE SHARE.

Strictly personal obligation. An OBLIGATION that "can be enforced only by the OBLIGEE, or only against the OBLIGOR," *viz.*, not against the obligor's successor and not by the obligee's successor. La. C.C. art. 1766. When a performance requires special a skill or quality of the obligor or when the performance is a personal service, the obligation is presumed to be strictly personal. *Id.* Likewise, a performance intended for the benefit of the obligee exclusively is strictly personal with respect to the obligee. *Id.*

Obligee. A creditor who may demand a performance of an OBLIGOR pursuant to an OBLIGATION. *See* La. C.C. art. 1756; *see also id.*, Comment (c).

Obligor. A debtor who is bound to render a performance to an OBLIGEE pursuant to an OBLIGATION. *See* La. C.C. art. 1756; *see also id.*, Comment (c).

Oblique action. An action whereby a creditor exercises a certain right available to the debtor when the debtor causes or increases his insolvency by failing to exercise that right. A creditor may not exercise a right that is STRICTLY PERSONAL to the debtor. *See* OBLIGATION, STRICTLY PERSONAL OBLIGATION; REVOCATORY ACTION.

For example, in *Succession of Quartararo*, a creditor of a potential heir accepted a succession on the heir's behalf through the use of the oblique action. 541 So.2d 243, 243 (La. App. 4 Cir. 1989).

Occupancy. The "taking of POSSESSION of a CORPOREAL MOVABLE that does not belong to anyone" whereby the occupant acquires OWNERSHIP of the THING. La. C.C. art. 3412.

Offer.

Irrevocable offer. "An offer that specifies a period of time for acceptance." La. C.C. art. 1928. Alternatively, an offeror may tacitly make an offer irrevocable for a reasonable period of time if he "manifests and intent to give the offeree a delay within which to accept, without specifying a time." *Id.* During this time, the offeror may not revoke the offer. *Contrast* OFFER, REVOCABLE OFFER.

Revocable offer. An offer that may be revoked at any time before its acceptance. La. C.C. art. 1930. *Contrast* OFFER, IRREVOCABLE OFFER.

Offres réelles. *French.* Literally, "real tender." A TENDER.

Olographic testament. *See* TESTAMENT, OLOGRAPHIC TESTAMENT.

Onerous contract. *See* CONTRACT, ONEROUS CONTRACT.

Open mine doctrine. The doctrine that entitles a USUFRUCTUARY to use and enjoy "the landowner's rights in minerals as to mines or quarries actually worked at the time the USUFRUCT was created." La. Mineral Code art. 190(A). The usufruct of a surviving spouse grants the usufructuary the right to use and enjoy the landowner's mineral rights even as to mines and quarries that were not open at the time the usufruct was created. *Id.* art. 190(B).

Ordinary repair. *See* REPAIR, ORDINARY REPAIR.

Out of commerce. A thing in which traffic is prohibited by law, e.g., scheduled narcotics and human organs. *See* La. C.C. art. 2448, Comment (b).

Ownership. The REAL RIGHT conferring on a person "direct, immediate, and exclusive authority over a THING. The owner of a thing may use, enjoy, and dispose of it within the limits and under the conditions established by law." La. C.C. art. 477(A). "Ownership exists independently of any exercise of it and may not be lost by nonuse." La. C.C. art. 481. It is, however, lost "when ACQUISITIVE PRESCRIPTION accrues in favor of an adverse possessor." *Id.* "Unless otherwise provided by law, the ownership of a tract of land carries with it the ownership of everything that is directly above or under it." La. C.C. art. 490.

> **Ownership in indivision.** The "ownership of the same THING by two or more persons." La. C.C. art. 797. Each CO-OWNER has the full use of the thing. Ownership in indivision

may be terminated by PARTITION of the property. The common law concepts of tenancy in common and joint tenancy are similar to ownership in indivision.

P

Pact de non alienando. A clause in a MORTGAGE giving the MORTGAGEE the right to foreclose by executory process directed solely against the MORTGAGOR, and giving the mortgagee the right to seize and sell the mortgaged property, regardless of any subsequent alienations. For example, such a clause might read "The mortgagors hereby agree in solido not to sell, alienate, deteriorate, or encumber said mortgaged property to the prejudice of the mortgage." Also called a non-alienation pact. *See* HYPOTHECARY ACTION.

Pacte de preference. A right of preemption. The equivalent of a right of FIRST REFUSAL.

Paraph. A signature by a notary on the evidence of an obligation, typically a COLLATERAL MORTGAGE NOTE, identifying the note with the COLLATERAL MORTGAGE securing the note. The phrase "NE VARIETUR" is traditionally used in the paraph. Paraphing is no longer required for EXECUTORY PROCESS.

The collateral mortgage will typically recite that the collateral note "has been paraphed 'ne varietur' for identification with the act." The paraph itself, appearing at the end of the collateral mortgage note, can read as follows.

Ne Varietur

For identification with an Act of Mortgage, dated the Fourteenth day of June, 1982, passed before me, the undersigned Notary.

Parish. A Louisiana governmental subdivision equivalent to a county in the other states.

Partition. An action for the division of property owned or bequeathed in INDIVISION. *See* La. C.C. arts. 1307, 1308, 807.

Definitive partition. A permanent and irrevocable PARTITION. La. C.C. art. 1295. The phrase can also refer to a judicial partition made according to law. La. C.C. art. 1296.

Judicial partition. A PARTITION made by a court.

Partition by licitation. The SALE of a THING owned in INDIVISION at public auction and the distribution of the proceeds among the former CO-OWNERS in proportion to their prior ownership interest. La. C.C. art. 811.

Partition by private sale. The SALE of a THING owned in INDIVISION privately and without public auction followed by the distribution of the proceeds among the former CO-OWNERS in proportion to their prior ownership interest. La. C.C. art. 811.

Partition in kind. A PARTITION in which the property is divided into discrete units of approximately equal worth, which are then distributed to the former CO-OWNERS in proportion to their former ownership interest. La. C.C. art. 810. Partition in kind is only available when the value of the divided pieces is about the same as the value of the whole, undivided THING. For example, if several co-owners own a large tract of land in indivision, it could be divided into lots and partitioned in kind.

Partition of a succession. The division of the decedent's ESTATE among the coheirs according to their rights. La. C.C. art. 1293.

Provisional partition. The PARTITION of either "certain things before the rest can be divided" or "of everything that is to be divided[] when the parties are not in a situation to make an irrevocable partition." La. C.C. art. 1295. Alternatively, a partition in which the required formalities have not been performed or "by which the parties are not definitively bound." La. C.C. art. 1296.

For example, a married couple may provisionally partition their community assets near the beginning of the divorce proceedings and then enter into a DEFINITIVE PARTITION after the divorce is completed.

Partnership. A JURIDICAL PERSON created by CONTRACT between two or more partners "to combine their efforts or resources in determined proportions and to collaborate at mutual risk for their common profit or commercial benefit." La. C.C. art. 2801.

> **Commercial partnership.** *Obsolete.* A partnership formed for buying, selling, or manufacture of goods or for the transportation of goods or people. La. C.C. art. 2825 (1870). *Contrast* PARTNERSHIP, ORDINARY PARTNERSHIP.
>
> The 1980 revision abolished the distinction between commercial and ordinary partnerships. La. C.C. art. 2814; *id.*, Comment (a).

> **Ordinary partnership.** *Obsolete.* A partnership that is not a COMMERCIAL PARTNERSHIP. La. C.C. art. 2826 (1870). *Contrast* PARTNERSHIP, COMMERCIAL PARTNERSHIP.
>
> The 1980 revision abolished the distinction between commercial and ordinary partnerships. La. C.C. art. 2814; *id.*, Comment (a).

> **Partnership in commendam.** A limited partnership which has "one or more general partners who have the powers, rights, and obligations of [full] partners" and one or more partners in commendam, whose liability is limited to the amount of their contribution to the partnership but who have no managerial, administrative, or binding authority on the partnership. La. C.C. arts. 2837, 2840, 2843.

Patrimony. The "sum total of a person's assets and liabilities." YIANNOPOULOS, 4 LA. CIVIL LAW TREATISE § 190. "Every person has [exactly one] patrimony and only a person may have a patrimony." *Id.* § 194.

Paulian action. A REVOCATORY ACTION.

Pawn. *See* PLEDGE, PAWN.

Payment. *Obligations.* The "performance of an OBLIGATION to pay money or to give fungible THINGS." La. C.C. art. 1864, Comment (b).

Pedis possessio. *Latin.* Literally, "possession by feet." Actual POSSESSION of land without the use of enclosures. La. C.C. art. 3426, Comment (d).

Penal clause. A "secondary OBLIGATION which can be enforced only if there is also a valid primary obligation which the OBLIGOR fails to perform without lawful excuse." La. C.C. art. 1808, Comment (d). *Contrast* OBLIGATION, ALTERNATIVE OBLIGATION.

Peremption. A "period of time fixed by law for the existence of a right." La. C.C. art. 3458. Unlike LIBERATIVE PRESCRIPTION, which merely prevents the enforcement of a right by judicial action, peremption extinguishes the right itself. *Id.;* La. C.C. art. 3447. Also, unlike liberative prescription, peremption may not be renounced, interrupted, or suspended. *Id.* art. 3461. *Contrast* PRESCRIPTION, LIBERATIVE PRESCRIPTION.

Peremptory exception. *See* EXCEPTION, PEREMPTORY EXCEPTION.

Perfect usufruct. *See* USUFRUCT, PERFECT USUFRUCT.

Performance. The act of "giving, doing, or not doing something." La. C.C. art. 1756.

Person.

> **Juridical person.** An "entity to which the law attributes personality, such as a corporation or a partnership. The personality of a juridical person is distinct from that of its members." La. C.C. art. 24.

> **Natural person.** A human being born alive. La. C.C. arts. 24–25.

Personal. Of or relating to a NATURAL or JURIDICAL PERSON.

> **Personal obligation.** *See* OBLIGATION, STRICTLY PERSONAL OBLIGATION.

> **Personal right.** The "legal power that a person (OBLIGEE) has to demand from another person (OBLIGOR) a performance consisting of giving, doing, or not doing a thing." YIANNOPOULOS, 4 LA. CIVIL LAW TREATISE § 203.

Personal servitude. *See* SERVITUDE, PERSONAL SERVITUDE.

Petitory action. *See* REAL ACTION, PETITORY ACTION.

Pledge. An ACCESSORY "CONTRACT by which one debtor gives something to his creditor as a security for his debt." La. C.C. art. 3133. There are two species of pledge: PAWN and ANTICHRESIS. La. C.C. art. 3134.

> **Pawn.** A PLEDGE in which a MOVABLE is given as security. La. C.C. art. 3135. Any movable susceptible of alienation or assignment—whether it is corporeal or incorporeal—may be pawned. La. C.C. arts. 3154–3156.

> **Antichresis.** A PLEDGE in which an IMMOVABLE is given as security. La. C.C. art. 3135.

Port-forte. *French.* The OBLIGOR in a PROMESSE DE PORTE-FORT, a person who, similar to a SURETY, is bound if the third party to the CONTRACT fails to render a performance that is the object of the promesse de porte-fort. La. C.C. art. 1977, Comment (b).

Possesseur précaire. *French.* Literally, a "precarious possessor." *See* POSSESSION, PRECARIOUS POSSESSION.

Possession. The "detention or enjoyment of a CORPOREAL THING, MOVABLE or IMMOVABLE, that one holds or exercises by himself or by another who keeps or exercises it in [the POSSESSOR's] name." La. C.C. art. 3421.

> **Civil possession.** The "retention of POSSESSION of a THING merely by virtue of the intent to own it, as when a person, without intending to abandon possession, ceases to reside in a house or on the land which he previously occupied or when a person ceases to exercise physical control over a MOVABLE without intending to abandon possession." La. C.C. art. 3431; *id.*, Comment (c).

> **Clandestine possession.** POSSESSION that "is not open or public." La. C.C. art. 3436.

Constructive possession. POSSESSION to the limits of the IMMOVABLE described in the TITLE by which a person possesses that immovable. La. C.C. art. 3426. Constructive possession only applies when the possessor has title to the immovable. For example, if a person has title to ten acres of ground but farms only one of the acres without setting foot on the rest, he constructively possesses the entire ten acres described in the title.

Corporeal possession. The "exercise of physical acts of use, detention, or enjoyment over a THING." La. C.C. art. 3425.

Discontinuous possession. Possession that is not exercised at regular intervals. La. C.C. art. 3436.

Equivocal possession. POSSESSION regarding which "there is ambiguity as to the intent of the possessor to own the thing." La. C.C. art. 3436.

Interruption of possession. The loss of POSSESSION—i.e., the abandonment of possession or EVICTION of the POSSESSOR. La. C.C. art. 3433–3434.

Precarious possession. POSSESSION exercised "over a THING with the permission or on behalf of the owner or POSSESSOR." La. C.C. art. 3437.

Quasi-possession. "The exercise of a REAL RIGHT, such as a SERVITUDE, with the intent to have it as one's own." La. C.C. art. 3421.

Vice of possession. *See* VICE, VICE OF POSSESSION.

Violent possession. POSSESSION "acquired or maintained by violent acts," so long as the violence persists. La. C.C. art. 3436.

Possessor. One who exercises POSSESSION of a THING.

Possessor in good faith. *Accession.* A POSSESSOR who "possesses by virtue of an ACT TRANSLATIVE OF TITLE" and who is ignorant of any defect in his ownership. La. C.C. art. 487. His good faith ends when he learns of a defect or an action is instituted against him for the recovery of the THING by its owner. *Id.*

Precarious possessor. One who exercises PRECARIOUS POSSESSION.

Possessory action. *See* REAL ACTION, POSSESSORY ACTION.

Potestative condition. *See* CONDITION, POTESTATIVE CONDITION.

Precarious possession. *See* POSSESSION, PRECARIOUS POSSESSION.

Predial servitude. *See* SERVITUDE, PREDIAL SERVITUDE.

Preference, lawful causes of. PRIVILEGE and MORTGAGE. La. C.C. art. 3184.

Preparatory act. *See* ACT, PREPARATORY ACT.

Prescription.

> **Acquisitive prescription.** A "mode of acquiring OWNERSHIP [of a THING] by POSSESSION for a period of time." La. C.C. art. 3446. Acquisitive prescription is similar to the common law concept of adverse possession.

> **Interruption of prescription.** An event that stops a prescriptive period from running and, when the interruption ceases, causes the prescriptive period to begin running anew. La. C.C. art. 3466. For example, ACQUISITIVE PRESCRIPTION is interrupted when POSSESSION is lost. La. C.C. art. 3465.

> **Liberative prescription.** A "mode of barring actions as a result of inaction for a period of time." La. C.C. art. 3447. Similar to the statute of limitations. Liberative prescription terminates the right to enforce the act by legal action, but does not terminate the NATURAL OBLIGATION that remains. *Brumfield v. McElwee*, 976 So.2d 234, 241 (La. App. 4 Cir. 2008). *Contrast* PEREMPTION.

Prescription of nonuse. A "mode of [extinguishing] a REAL RIGHT other than ownership as a result of failure to exercise the right for a period of time." La. C.C. art. 3448. SERVITUDES, for example, can be extinguished through the prescription of nonuse.

Renunciation of prescription. The "abandonment of rights derived from an accrual of PRESCRIPTION." La. C.C. art. 3449, Comment (c). Renunciation may be express or tacit. *Id.* art. 3450. Renunciation of ACQUISITIVE PRESCRIPTION of MOVABLES must be express to be effective. *Id. Contrast* ACKNOWLEDGMENT.

Suspension of prescription. An event that stops a prescriptive period from accruing during the suspensive period. La. C.C. art. 3472. After the suspensive period is over, the accrual of PRESCRIPTION resumes. *Id.* Similar to the tolling of a statute of limitations, prescription may be suspended in certain situations, for example, as between spouses during the marriage. La. C.C. art. 3469.

Prescription of nonuse. *See* PRESCRIPTION, PRESCRIPTION OF NONUSE.

Price. *Sales.* A fixed sum of money, either certain or determinable by a designated method, that is proportionate to the value of the THING sold. La. C.C. art. 2464.

Principal contract. *See* CONTRACT, PRINCIPAL CONTRACT.

Principal obligation. *See* OBLIGATION, PRINCIPAL OBLIGATION.

Principal thing. *See* THING, PRINCIPAL THING.

Prior in tempore, potior in jure. *Latin.* Literally, "first in time, greater in right." The principle that rights are subject to temporal priority. For example, a prior MORTGAGE takes precedence over a subsequent USUFRUCT. *See* La. C.C. art. 620, Comment (b).

Private road. *See* ROAD, PRIVATE ROAD.

Private thing. *See* THING, PRIVATE THING.

Privilege. A right given to certain creditors of a debtor that entitles them to be paid before the debtor's other creditors, including those with MORTGAGES. La. C.C. art. 3186. Privileges include, e.g., FUNERAL CHARGES, charges incurred during a decedent's LAST SICKNESS, and court costs. La. C.C. arts. 3191, 3195.

Proces verbal. A transcript of a hearing, such as a probate hearing, signed by a judge or clerk.

Procuration. A "unilateral JURIDICAL ACT by which a person, the principal, confers authority on another person, the representative, to represent the principal in legal relations." La. C.C. art. 2987. *Compare* MANDATARY.

Product. *Property.* A THING derived from another "thing as a result of diminution of its substance," e.g., harvested timber or mined coal. La. C.C. art. 488.

    Products liability. Industrial products and "natural substances, whether raw, processed, or otherwise altered by the industry of man." La. C.C. art. 3545, Comment (a). "A product may be MOVABLE or IMMOVABLE, a single or a composite thing, and includes its COMPONENT PARTS." *Id.*

Prohibited substitution. *See* SUBSTITUTION, PROHIBITED SUBSTITUTION.

Promesse de porte-fort. *French.* A CONTRACT that has as its object

> an act to be done by another party. [It] is a security device that resembles SURETYSHIP in that the promisee, or PORTE-FORT, is bound only if the third person does not satisfy the obligee, but differs from suretyship in that the promisor never becomes an accessory obligor. For as long as the third person does not bind himself, the promisor remains the sole obligor, and as soon as the third person binds himself the promisor is released.

La. C.C. art. 1977, Comment (b); *see, generally,* La. C.C. art. 1977.

Promise of sale. *See* SALE, PROMISE OF SALE.

Property. The "word 'property' in [the current] revision [of the Civil Code] is at times used to mean THINGS ... and at times to mean PATRIMONY." La. C.C. art. 2325, Comment (b).

Propinquity of sanguinity. *Successions.* The number of DEGREES or generations separating two COLLATERALS who share a common ancestor. The number of degrees is equal to the number of generations between the HEIR and the common ancestor plus the number of generations between the common ancestor and the deceased. La. C.C. art. 900.

Propter rem. *Latin.* Literally, "on account of the thing." For example, a REAL OBLIGATION is *propter rem*, *viz.*, it "follows the immovable in the hands of every successor." La. C.C. art. 746, Comment (b).

Prudent administrator. The English analog to the French BON PÈRE DE FAMILLE and the Roman *paterfamilias*. A prudent administrator "is liable even for the slightest fault [in the thing he is administering], namely he must exercise the diligence that an attentive and careful man exercises in the management of his own affairs." La. C.C. art. 576, Comment (b). For example, a USUFRUCTUARY must act as a prudent administrator in caring for the property burdened by the USUFRUCT. *See* La. C.C. arts. 576–577.

Prudent owner. *See* PRUDENT ADMINISTRATOR.

Public road. *See* ROAD, PUBLIC ROAD.

Public thing. *See* THING, PUBLIC THING.

Putative marriage. *See* MARRIAGE, PUTATIVE MARRIAGE.

Putative title. A TITLE that is believed to exist but that, in reality, does not. La. C.C. art. 3483, Comment (e). A putative title does not constitute a JUST TITLE for purposes of article 3483.

Q

Quasi-possession. *See* POSSESSION, QUASI-POSSESSION.

Quitclaim deed. A transfer to another of whatever rights in a THING a person has without guaranteeing the existence of any such rights. La. C.C. 2502.

R

Ratification. A "declaration whereby a person gives his consent to an OBLIGATION incurred on his behalf by another without his authority." La. C.C. art. 1843.

> **Express ratification.** A JURIDICAL ACT evidencing a party's "intention to be bound by the ratified OBLIGATION." La. C.C. art. 1843.

> **Tacit ratification.** A RATIFICATION in which a person accepts the benefits of the OBLIGATION with knowledge that it was incurred on his behalf by another. La. C.C. art. 1843.

Real. Of or relating to property. *Contrast* PERSONAL.

Real action. An action for the enforcement of a REAL RIGHT, i.e., "ownership, personal and predial servitudes, and real security." YIANNOPOULOS, 4 LA. CIVIL LAW TREATISE § 241.

> **Boundary action.** An imprescriptible and nominate REAL ACTION available to an owner, USUFRUCTUARY, or LESSEE of an IMMOVABLE for the judicial determination of the boundaries of the immovable. La. C.C. art. 788. *See* FIXING OF THE BOUNDARY; NOMINATE ACTION.

> **Confessory action.** An innominate REAL "ACTION for the recognition of a SERVITUDE on another's IMMOVABLE." YIANNOPOULOS, 4 LA. CIVIL LAW TREATISE § 241. *See, also,* INNOMINATE ACTION.

Hypothecary action. An innominate REAL ACTION whereby a MORTGAGEE takes POSSESSION of the mortgaged property for the purpose of subjecting it to judicial SALE. *See* YIANNOPOULOS, 4 LA. CIVIL LAW TREATISE § 291.

Negatory action. An innominate REAL "ACTION for injunction against an attempted exercise of a PREDIAL SERVITUDE." YIANNOPOULOS, 4 LA. CIVIL LAW TREATISE § 241.

Petitory action. A REAL ACTION brought by an owner of an IMMOVABLE of which he is not in POSSESSION against the current POSSESSOR for the recognition of the former's OWNERSHIP over the property. La. C.C.P. art. 3651.

Possessory action. A nominate REAL ACTION brought by the POSSESSOR of an IMMOVABLE against someone who has disturbed his POSSESSION for the recognition of the former's right to possess the THING and to restore his possession. La. C.C.P. art. 3655.

Revendication. An innominate REAL ACTION available to an owner for the recovery of a MOVABLE THING and for the recognition of his OWNERSHIP of it. La. C.C. art. 526, Comment (b); YIANNOPOULOS, 4 LA. CIVIL LAW TREATISE § 241; *id.* § 350. *Compare* REAL ACTION, PETITORY ACTION.

Real obligation. *See* OBLIGATION, REAL OBLIGATION.

Real right. A right conferring direct and immediate authority over a THING, whether MOVABLE or IMMOVABLE. "Real right" is sometimes erroneously associated solely with a right in immovable property. Examples include OWNERSHIP and PERSONAL and PREDIAL SERVITUDES. *See* OBLIGATION, REAL OBLIGATION.

Accessory real right. A REAL RIGHT accessory to the OBLIGATION it secures, including "PLEDGES, chattel mortgages, special PRIVILEGES or liens, and other security interests." La. C.C. art. 3536, Comment (a).

Emphyteusis. *See* RENT OF LANDS.

Habitation. "[T]he nontransferable REAL RIGHT of a NATURAL PERSON to dwell in the house of another." La. C.C. art. 630. The extent and duration of the right are defined by the title that creates it, La. C.C. art. 632; Louisiana Civil Code articles 633–635 provide suppletive rules that govern in the absence of contractual provisions.

Principal real right. A REAL RIGHT that pertains "to the substance of the THING," i.e., OWNERSHIP and its dismemberments. La. C.C. art. 3536, Comment (a). *Contrast* REAL RIGHT, ACCESSORY REAL RIGHT.

Right of first refusal. *See* FIRST REFUSAL, RIGHT OF.

Right of use. A PERSONAL SERVITUDE conferring "in favor of a person a specified use of an estate less than full enjoyment." La. C.C. art. 639. Similar to the common law's right of way, privilege, easements in gross, or profits in gross.

Right to possess. The right to POSSESS a thing by virtue of having possessed it as owner for more than a year. La. C.C. art. 3422.

Servitude. *See* SERVITUDE.

Usufruct. *See* USUFRUCT.

Real subrogation. The principle by which a new THING takes the place of the thing it replaces. For example, real subrogation "is applicable to both SEPARATE and COMMUNITY PROPERTY. Thus, when a thing forming a part of the separate property of a spouse is converted into another thing, the mass of the separate property is not diminished. The new thing takes the place of the old." La. C.C. art. 2341, Comment (c).

Real tender. *See* TENDER.

Reasonable effort. *Obligations*. An effort that does "not place an excessive burden on the" actor. La. C.C. art. 2002, Comment (c). For example, an "OBLIGEE must make reasonable efforts to mitigate the damage caused by the OBLIGOR's failure to perform." La. C.C. art. 2002.

Reciprocal obligations. Those OBLIGATIONS arising from BILATERAL or SYNALLAGMATIC CONTRACTS. La. C.C. art. 1993, Comment (b).

Reconduction of a lease. The continuation of an expired LEASE by the LESSEE'S continued POSSESSION of the leased property. The reconducted lease retains the same provisions as the original, with the exception of its term. La. C.C. art. 2724. The length of the additional term is determined by articles 2722 and 2723.

Reconventional demand. A judicial demand asserted by the petition of a defendant in an action against the plaintiff, regardless of the connection between the two demands. La. C.C.P. art. 1061. Also called a demand in reconvention.

Redemption. *Sales.* The right a seller may reserve to take back the THING sold by repaying the purchase price. La. C.C. art. 2567.

Redhibition. The rescission of a SALE or a reduction in the sale price on account of a REDHIBITORY DEFECT in the THING sold. La. C.C. art. 2520. Redhibition is sought in an action for redhibition or redhibitory action.

Redhibitory defect. A defect in a THING that "renders the thing useless" or renders "its use so inconvenient that it must be presumed a buyer would not have bought the thing had he known of the defect." La. C.C. art. 2520. A defect is also redhibitory when "it diminishes the [thing's] usefulness or its value so that it must be presumed that a buyer would still have bought it but for a lesser price." *Id.*

Rejection of goods. *Sales.* The right of a buyer to "reject nonconforming THINGS within a reasonable time" by giving reasonable notice to the seller of the rejection. La. C.C. art. 2605.

Relative nullity. *See* NULLITY, RELATIVE NULLITY.

Relative simulation. *See* SIMULATION, RELATIVE SIMULATION.

Relatively null marriage. *See* MARRIAGE, RELATIVELY NULL MARRIAGE.

Relativity of contracts. The principle that CONTRACTS "may produce effects for third parties only when provided by law." La. C.C. art. 1985; *id.*, Comment (a).

Remunerative donation. *See* DONATION, REMUNERATIVE DO-
NATION.

Rent. The performance given by a LESSEE in return for leasing a
THING. "The rent may consist of [giving] money, commodities,
FRUITS, services, or other PERFORMANCES sufficient to support an
ONEROUS CONTRACT." La. C.C. art. 2675. *See* LEASE.

Rent of Lands. A "CONTRACT by which one of the parties conveys
and cedes to the other a [tract] of land, or any other IMMOVABLE
property, and stipulates that the latter shall hold it as owner, but
reserving to the former an annual rent of a certain sum of money,
or of a certain quantity of fruits, which the other party binds
himself to pay him." La. C.C. art. 2779. The contract shares
elements of both SALE and LEASE. *Id.* art. 2782. The obligation to
pay rent is perpetual and runs with the land. *Id.* art. 2786.
However, the rent charge may be redeemed by paying the
redemption price, which may be stipulated in the contract or
determined by the value of the land. *Id.* arts. 2788, 2790. *See,
generally,* Gregory W. Rome, *An Elegy for Emphyteusis,* 1 CIV. L.
COMMENTARIES no. 2, p. 1 (2008), at http://www.law.tulane.edu
/uploadedFiles/Institutes_and_Centers/Eason_Weinmann/v01i
02-Rome.pdf.

Renunciation of prescription. *See* PRESCRIPTION, RENUNCIA-
TION OF PRESCRIPTION.

Renunciation of succession. *See* SUCCESSION, RENUNCIATION OF
SUCCESSION.

Renvoi. *French.* Literally, "remission." The principle that a court
should take into account the law of conflict of laws of a foreign
state when the rest of the law of that state is applicable. *See* La.
C.C. art. 3517; *id.,* Comment (a).

Repairs.

> **Extraordinary repairs.** *Usufruct.* Repairs "for the re-
> construction of the whole or of a substantial part of the
> property subject to USUFRUCT." La. C.C. art. 578. The NAKED
> OWNER is responsible for making extraordinary repairs. *Id.*
> art. 577.

Ordinary repairs. *Usufruct.* REPAIRS that are not EXTRA-ORDINARY REPAIRS. La. C.C. art. 578. The USUFRUCTUARY is responsible for making ordinary repairs. *Id.* art. 577.

Repetition. A demand or action for the return of money or a THING that was paid but that was not due.

Representation. The methods by which one person may take the place of another person in legal relations, whether that authority is "conferred by law[;] by CONTRACT, such as MANDATE or PARTNERSHIP[;] or by the unilateral JURIDICAL ACT of PROCURATION." La. C.C. art. 2986; *id.* art. 2985, Comment (b). Representation is the civilian analog of common law agency. *Id.*, Comment (a).

Res nullius. *Latin.* Literally, "a thing belonging to no one." A THING that is owned by no one, e.g., wild animals and abandoned things. La. C.C. art. 3412, Comment (d).

Resiliation. *French.* Dissolution of a CONTRACT without retroactive effect. For example, performance under the contracts of lease or for insurance cannot be undone, so their dissolution operates only prospectively. *See* La. C.C. art. 2019, Comment (d).

Resolutory condition. *See* CONDITION, RESOLUTORY CONDITION.

Resolutory term. *See* TERM, RESOLUTORY TERM.

Respite. An "ACT by which a debtor, who is unable to satisfy his debts at the moment, transacts with his creditors and obtains from them additional time for the payment of the debt." La. C.C. art. 3084.

> **Forced respite.** A proposal for RESPITE refused by some of the creditors who are then forced to accept it by the judgment of a court. La. C.C. art. 3085.

> **Voluntary respite.** A proposal for RESPITE to which all the creditors have consented. La. C.C. art. 3085.

Retail dealer. A person who keeps "an open shop[] and sell[s], by small portions, provisions and liquor." La. C.C. art. 3208.

Revendication. *See* REAL ACTION, REVENDICATION.

Revendicatory action. *See* REAL ACTION, REVENDICATION.

Revocable offer. *See* OFFER, REVOCABLE OFFER.

Revocation.

> **Particular revocation.** *Successions.* The revocation of certain testamentary dispositions but not others. La. C.C. art. 1691 (1870). The code article defining the particular revocation was replaced in the revision by La. C.C. art. 1608, entitled "[r]evocation of a LEGACY or other testamentary provision."

> **Revocation of a testament.** *Successions.* The revocation of an entire TESTAMENT by physically destroying it or having it destroyed, by declaring its revocation "in a one of the forms prescribed for testaments or in an AUTHENTIC ACT," or by identifying and clearly revoking "the testament by a writing signed by the TESTATOR in his own handwriting." La. C.C. art. 1607.

Revocatory action. An action by which an OBLIGEE enforces his right "to annul an act of the OBLIGOR, or the result of a failure to act of the obligor, made or effected after the right of the obligee arose, that causes or increases the obligee's insolvency." La. C.C. art. 2036. The action is analogous to the common law's suit to set aside a fraudulent conveyance. *Id.*, Comment (b). *See, also,* OBLIQUE ACTION.

Right of first refusal. *See* FIRST REFUSAL, RIGHT OF.

Right of use. *See* SERVITUDE, RIGHT OF USE.

Right to possess. *See* REAL RIGHT, RIGHT TO POSSESS.

Road.

> **Private road.** A road not subject to public use. La. C.C. art. 457.

> **Public road.** A road subject to public use. La. C.C. art. 457.

Rule of validation. *Conflict of laws.* A principle that favors the upholding of a "TESTAMENT as to form if it conforms to the pertinent requirements of any state that is sufficiently related with the deceased and his testament." La. C.C. art. 3528, Comment (c); *see id.* art. 3528.

S

Sale. A NOMINATE CONTRACT whereby one "transfers OWNERSHIP of a THING to another for a PRICE in money." La. C.C. art. 2439. Once the parties have determined the thing and the price and have consented to the sale, it is perfected and ownership is transferred. *Id.*; and *id.* art. 2456.

> **Lump sale.** A SALE in which a definite group of THINGS is priced and sold as a single unit. La. C.C. art. 2458. The sale is complete upon the parties' consent, even if the things have not yet been weighed, counted, or measured to determine whether the seller complied with the contract. *Id.*
>
> For example, a sale of all the wine in Arpent Noir's cellar for $5,000 is a lump sale. Such a sale is perfected when the vendor and vendee agree to sell the lot for the price.
>
> **Option to buy or sell.** A NOMINATE CONTRACT whereby one party gives the other the right to accept an offer to buy or sell a thing within a certain amount of time. La. C.C. art. 2620. This contract is a particular species of OPTION CONTRACT.
>
> **Promise of sale.** "An agreement whereby one party promises to sell and the other promises to buy a THING at a later time, or upon the happening of a condition, or upon performance of some OBLIGATION by either party." La. C.C. art. 2623. The CONTRACT must name the thing to be sold, its PRICE, and must meet the formal requirements of a SALE of that type of thing. *Id.*
>
> **Sale by weight, tale, or measure.** A SALE in which the PRICE of the goods is determined by the weight, count, or measure of the goods sold. La. C.C. art. 2458. The sale is

perfected and OWNERSHIP transferred when the seller counts, weighs, or measures the THINGS with the buyer's consent. *Id.*

Sale of a future thing. The SALE of a THING that does not yet exist. Such a sale is subject to a SUSPENSIVE CONDITION that the thing does actually come into existence. La. C.C. art. 2450.

Sale of a hope. The SALE of an uncertain hope, e.g., a fisherman selling a haul of his net before throwing it. La. C.C. art. 2451. The CONTRACT transfers OWNERSHIP of the realized THINGS according to the expectations of the parties. *Id.*

Sale of litigious rights. The SALE of a right that is contested in a lawsuit already filed. *See* La. C.C. art. 2652. LITIGIOUS RIGHTS may not be sold to the officers of the court in which the right is contested. *Id.* art. 2447. With the exception of rights sold to a co-obligor, an OBLIGEE may extinguish the litigious right that has been sold by paying the asignee the price he paid to purchase it. *Id.* art. 2652.

Sale on view or trial. A SALE in which the buyer reserves his right to view or try the object of the sale and conditions his acceptance upon his satisfaction with it. La. C.C. art. 2460.

Sale per aversionem. A SALE of an IMMOVABLE that is designated by reference to its boundaries and sold for a lump PRICE without regard to the area of the land. For example, a contract to sell a tract of land bounded by the Mississippi River, the river road, Arpent Noir, and Arpent Blanc for $10,000 is a sale per aversionem. *See* La. C.C. art. 2495. *Contrast* SALE, SALE BY WEIGHT, TALE, OR MEASURE.

Sealed testament. *Obsolete. See* TESTAMENT, MYSTIC TESTAMENT.

Seashore. The "land on which the waters of the sea spread in the highest tide during the winter season." La. C.C. art. 451.

Seizin. POSSESSION and OWNERSHIP of the estate of a decedent that is transferred to his HEIRS and LEGATEES at the moment of his death. *See* La. C.C. art. 935. A successor's exercise of his rights in his inheritance are subject to administration of the estate by the succession representative once one has qualified. La. C.C. art. 938.

Separate property. Property belonging to one spouse exclusively, i.e., that which is not COMMUNITY PROPERTY. La. C.C. art. 2341 contains a more detailed listing of what property is separate, but the category commonly includes things like property acquired by a spouse before the marriage, property acquired with other separate property, a spouse's inheritance, and donations made to one spouse alone. Community property that is PARTITIONED becomes the separate property of the spouse who acquires it.

Separation of property regime. A regime "established by a MATRIMONIAL AGREEMENT that excludes the legal regime of COMMUNITY OF ACQUETS AND GAINS or [established] by a judgment decreeing separation of property." La. C.C. art. 2370. Under this regime, some or all of the rules of the community of acquets and gains are suspended, *viz.*, some property that would ordinarily have been classified as COMMUNITY PROPERTY (e.g., spouses' earnings) will be classified as SEPARATE PROPERTY.

Often the separate property regime is created by MATRIMONIAL AGREEMENT, but under certain circumstances the regime may be created by judgment. For example, a spouse may seek a judgment decreeing separation of property if the other spouse's neglect or incompetence will diminish the first spouse's interest. *See* La. C.C. art. 2374.

Sequestration. The delivery of a THING to a third-party DEPOSITARY while the rights respecting the thing are determined. *See* La. C.C. art. 2946.

> **Conventional sequestration.** SEQUESTRATION by agreement. La. C.C. art. 2946. The DEPOSITARY is bound to deliver the sequestered THING in accordance with the parties' agreement or by court order. *Id.*

> **Judicial sequestration.** SEQUESTRATION by court order. La. C.C. art. 2949. A writ of sequestration may issue when "one claims the OWNERSHIP or right to POSSESSION of property, or a MORTGAGE, security interest, lien, or PRIVILEGE thereon" if the defendant can waste, conceal, or dispose of the disputed property or its revenues while the action is

pending. La. C.C.P. art. 3571. *See, generally,* La. C.C.P. arts. 3571–3576.

Servant. For the purposes of the Civil Code, an employee who resides in the house of his employer. La. C.C. art. 3205.

Servient estate. *See* ESTATE, SERVIENT ESTATE.

Servitude. A charge on a THING in favor of either a person, as in the case of a PERSONAL SERVITUDE, or in favor of another estate, as in the case of a PREDIAL SERVITUDE.

> **Affirmative servitude.** A PREDIAL SERVITUDE "giv[ing] the right to the owner of the DOMINANT ESTATE to do a certain thing on the SERVIENT ESTATE." La. C.C. art. 706.

> **Apparent servitude.** A PREDIAL SERVITUDE that is perceivable by "exterior signs, works, or constructions," e.g., a road or a window in a common wall. La. C.C. art. 707.

> **Conventional servitude.** A SERVITUDE established by CONTRACT. *See* La. C.C. art. 654.

> **Legal servitude.** "[L]imitations on OWNERSHIP established by law for the benefit of the general public or for the benefit of particular persons," La. C.C. art. 659, e.g., the OBLIGATION to keep one's building in repair so that it does not fall and cause damage to a neighbor or to a passerby. *See* YIANNOPOULOS, 4 LA. CIVIL LAW TREATISE § 23.

> **Mineral servitude.** A REAL RIGHT conveyed by a landowner to another allowing the latter to extract MINERALS from the SERVIENT ESTATE. Also called a mineral lease.

> **Natural servitude.** A PREDIAL SERVITUDE arising from the natural situation of the two estates, La. C.C. art. 654, e.g., the servitude of natural drainage. *Id.* art. 655.

> **Negative servitude.** A PREDIAL SERVITUDE "impos[ing] on the owner of the SERVIENT ESTATE the duty to abstain from doing something on his estate." La. C.C. art. 706.

Nonapparent servitude. A PREDIAL SERVITUDE without any outward sign of its existence, e.g., building restrictions. La. C.C. art. 707.

Personal servitude. "A charge on a THING for the benefit of a person." La. C.C. art. 534. The three major personal servitudes are USUFRUCT, HABITATION, and RIGHTS OF USE.

Predial servitude. A "charge on a SERVIENT ESTATE for the benefit of a DOMINANT ESTATE." La. C.C. art. 646. The two estates must be owned by different owners. Predial servitudes are either APPARENT or NONAPPARENT. Similar to an appurtenant easement at common law.

Servitude by destination. A PREDIAL SERVITUDE created by the prior establishment of a relationship between two estates owned by the same owner that would form a predial servitude if the estates belonged to different owners. When the two estates cease to belong to one owner, unless there is an express provision to the contrary, an apparent servitude comes into existence automatically, and a nonapparent servitude comes into existence if the owner previously filed in the registry a formal declaration establishing the servitude by destination. La. C.C. art. 741.

For example, where a person owns two adjacent lots and erects a building on one lot that encroaches on the other, the owner creates a servitude by destination that comes into existence when he alienates the encroached-upon lot. *See Carlon v. Marquart*, 10 So.2d 246 (La. App. Orleans 1942).

Servitude of light. The "right by which the owner of the DOMINANT ESTATE is entitled to make openings in a common wall for the admission of light; this includes the right to prevent the neighbor from making an obstruction." La. C.C. art. 703.

Servitude of passage. The right of persons, animals, and vehicles to pass through the SERVIENT ESTATE for the benefit of the DOMINANT ESTATE. La. C.C. art. 705.

Servitude of prohibition of light. The "right of the owner of the DOMINANT ESTATE to prevent his neighbor from making an opening in his own wall for the admission of light or that limits him to certain lights only." La. C.C. art. 704.

Servitude of prohibition of view. The "right of the owner of the DOMINANT ESTATE to prevent or limit openings of view on the SERVIENT ESTATE." La. C.C. art. 702.

Servitude of support. The "right by which buildings or other constructions of the DOMINANT ESTATE are permitted to rest on a wall of the SERVIENT ESTATE. Unless the title provides otherwise, the owner of the servient estate is bound to keep the wall fit for the exercise of the servitude, but he may be relieved of this charge by abandoning the wall." La. C.C. art. 700.

Servitude of view. The "right by which the owner of the DOMINANT ESTATE enjoys a view; this includes the right to prevent the raising of constructions on the SERVIENT ESTATE that would obstruct the view." La. C.C. art. 701.

Servitude by destination. *See* SERVITUDE, SERVITUDE BY DESTINATION.

Several obligation. *See* OBLIGATION, SEVERAL OBLIGATION.

Simulation. A CONTRACT that "does not express the true intent of the parties" by their mutual agreement. La. C.C. art. 2025. *See, also,* COUNTERLETTER.

Absolute simulation. A CONTRACT which the parties intend to have no effects between them. La. C.C. art. 2026.

Relative simulation. A SIMULATION in which "the parties intend that their CONTRACT shall produce effects between them though different from those recited in the contract." La. C.C. art. 2027.

Situs rule. A rule of conflict of laws stating that REAL RIGHTS in IMMOVABLES are to be determined by the laws of the state in which the immovable is located, i.e. the THING's situs. *See* La. C.C. art. 3535.

Solidary liability. Liability under a SOLIDARY OBLIGATION. Similar to the common law's joint and several liability.

Solidary obligation. *See* OBLIGATION, SOLIDARY OBLIGATION.

Special mortgage. *See* MORTGAGE, SPECIAL MORTGAGE.

Stipulated damages. "[D]amages to be recovered in case of nonperformance, defective performance, or delay of performance of an OBLIGATION" stipulated by the parties, normally in the CONTRACT giving rise to the obligation. La. C.C. art. 2005.

Stipulation pour autri. A stipulation in a CONTRACT of a benefit for a third person, the third-party beneficiary. La. C.C. art. 1978. Once the third-party beneficiary indicates that he wishes to enjoy the benefit, he must thereafter give his consent before the parties may dissolve the agreement. *Id.* The third-party beneficiary may demand performance of the OBLIGOR. *Id.* art. 1981.

Strictly personal obligation. *See* OBLIGATION, STRICTLY PERSONAL OBLIGATION.

Submission. A written "covenant by which persons who have a lawsuit or difference with one another[] name ARBITRATORS to decide the matter and bind themselves reciprocally to perform what [is] arbitrated." La. C.C. arts. 3099–3100.

Subrogation. The conventional or legal "substitution of one person to the rights of another." La. C.C. art. 1825. For example, when an insurer pays its insured for damages he sustained in an accident, the insurer is subrogated to the rights of its insured, *viz.,* the insurer may exercise the rights the insured had against the person who injured him. In effect, the insurer has paid what the tortfeasor owed their insured for the damage the tortfeasor caused and may then collect that amount from the tortfeasor. *See* La. C.C. arts. 1826–1830.

Substitute. *See* HEIR, SUBSTITUTED HEIR.

Substitute heir. *See* HEIR, SUBSTITUTE HEIR; SUBSTITUTION, PROHIBITED SUBSTITUTION.

Substitution. *See* FIDEICOMMISSARY SUBSTITUTION.

Prohibited substitution. "A disposition that is not in trust by which a THING is donated in full OWNERSHIP to a first donee, called the INSTITUTE, with a charge to preserve the thing and deliver it to a second donee, called the SUBSTITUTE, at the death of the institute." La. C.C. art. 1520. Such a DONATION is NULL.

This restriction on property transfers is known to the common law as the problem of mortmain or "dead hand" control, which the common law regulates by the rule against perpetuities.

See, generally, John H. Tucker, Jr., *Substitutions, Fideicommissa and Trusts in Louisiana Law: A Semantical Reappraisal,* 24 LA. L. REV. 439 (1964). *Contrast* SUBSTITUTION, VULGAR SUBSTITUTION.

Vulgar substitution. A "disposition by which a third person is called to take a gift or LEGACY in case the donee or LEGATEE does not take it." La. C.C. 1521. This type of substitution is valid. *Id. Contrast* SUBSTITUTION, PROHIBITED SUBSTITUTION.

Succession. The "transmission of the ESTATE of the deceased to his SUCCESSORS," who then may take possession of the estate according to law. La. C.C. art. 871.

Express acceptance of succession. *See* SUCCESSION, FORMAL ACCEPTANCE OF SUCCESSION.

Formal acceptance of succession. An acceptance of SUCCESSION rights by an express writing or by assuming the position of SUCCESSOR in a judicial proceeding. La. C.C. art. 957.

Informal acceptance of succession. An acceptance of SUCCESSION rights via "some act that clearly implies his intention to accept." La. C.C. art. 957.

Intestate succession. A SUCCESSION governed by the intestacy provisions of the civil code. La. C.C. art. 875. Intestate succession occurs in the absence of a TESTAMENT. *See* La. C.C. art. 874.

Partition of a succession. The division of the property of the decedent's ESTATE among the coheirs according to their rights at law or under the decedent's TESTAMENT. La. C.C. art. 1293.

Renunciation of succession. A SUCCESSOR's rejection of some or all the SUCCESSION rights to which he is entitled. *See* La. C.C. art. 947. Upon his rejection, the successor's rights ACCRETE to other successors. *Id.* arts. 964–965.

Testate succession. A SUCCESSION governed by "the will of the deceased, contained in a TESTAMENT executed in a form prescribed by law." La. C.C. art. 874.

Tacit acceptance of succession. *See* SUCCESSION, IN-FORMAL ACCEPTANCE OF SUCCESSION.

Vacant succession. A SUCCESSION that is claimed by no one, that has no known HEIRS, or that has been renounced by all known heirs. La. C.C. 1095.

Successor. A person who takes the place of another. La. C.C. art. 3506(28).

Intestate successor. An HEIR. La. C.C. art. 876.

Particular successor. A SUCCESSOR who "succeeds only to the rights appertaining to the THING which is sold, ceded or bequeathed to him." La. C.C. art. 3506(28).

Testate successor. A LEGATEE. La. C.C. 876.

Universal successor. A SUCCESSOR who "represents the person of the deceased[] and succeeds to all his rights and charges." La. C.C. art. 3506(28).

Suppletive law. General background law. It fills in gaps where, for example, a CONTRACT does not provide for a certain situation. However, the parties are free to derogate from the suppletive provisions by contract.

Suretyship. An "ACCESSORY CONTRACT by which a person binds himself to a creditor to fulfill the OBLIGATION of another upon the failure of the latter to do so." La. C.C. art. 3035.

Commercial suretyship. A SURETYSHIP in which the "surety is engaged in a surety business; ... [t]he principal OBLIGOR of the surety is a business corporation, partnership, or other business entity; ... [t]he principal obligation arises out of a commercial transaction of the principal obligor; or ... [t]he suretyship arises out of a commercial transaction of the surety." La. C.C. art. 3042.

Legal suretyship. SURETYSHIP given "pursuant to legislation, administrative act or regulation, or court order." La. C.C. art. 3043.

Ordinary suretyship. A SURETYSHIP that is neither commercial nor legal. La. C.C. art. 3044. *Contrast* SURETYSHIP, COMMERCIAL SURETYSHIP and LEGAL SURETYSHIP.

Suspension of prescription. *See* PRESCRIPTION, SUSPENSION OF PRESCRIPTION.

Suspensive appeal. *See* APPEAL, SUSPENSIVE APPEAL.

Suspensive condition. *See* CONDITION, SUSPENSIVE CONDITION.

Suspensive term. *See* TERM, SUSPENSIVE TERM.

Synallagmatic contract. *See* CONTRACT, SYNALLAGMATIC CONTRACT.

T

Tableau of distribution. *Successions.* A table showing the debts of the decedent's ESTATE and available funds. *See* La. C.C.P. art. 3033.

Tacit acceptance. *See* SUCCESSION, TACIT ACCEPTANCE.

Tacit renunciation. *See* PRESCRIPTION, RENUNCIATION OF PRESCRIPTION.

Tender. An "offer to perform according to the nature of the OBLI-GATION," La. C.C. art. 1869. If the performance consists of delivering a THING or paying money, tender requires the OBLIGOR produce the money or thing and place it at the immediate disposition of the OBLIGEE. LITVINOFF, 5 LA. CIVIL LAW TREATISE § 15.11; *see* La. C.C. art. 1869, Comment (g).

Term. A period of time for the performance of an OBLIGATION. La. C.C. art. 1778.

> **Certain term.** A fixed period of time for the performance of an OBLIGATION. La. C.C. art. 1778.

> **Resolutory term.** "The time given ... for the performance of an OBLIGATION." La. C.C. art. 1777, Comment (d); *id.* art. 2048 (1870).

> **Suspensive term.** "A term for the performance of an OBLIGATION." La. C.C. art. 1777; *id.*, Comment (d).

> **Uncertain term.** An uncertain period of time for the performance of an OBLIGATION that is either determinable by the intent of the parties or by the occurrence of an inevitable future event—e.g., the death of a person—or indeterminable, "in which case the obligation must be performed within a reasonable time." La. C.C. art. 1778.

Testament. A document disposing of the TESTATOR'S property *mortis causa* executed in a particular form. *See* La. C.C. art. 1570. Also called a will.

> **Mystic testament.** *Obsolete.* A TESTAMENT which is placed into a sealed envelope. Also called the secret, closed, or sealed testament.

> **Notarial testament.** A TESTAMENT executed in accordance with the requirements of Civil Code articles 1577–1580.1. Generally, the testament must be written; dated; signed by the TESTATOR, a notary, and two witnesses in front of one another; and must include an attestation clause signed by the notary and witnesses.

> **Nuncupative testament.** *Obsolete.* An oral TESTAMENT dictated by the TESTATOR in his LAST SICKNESS.

Olographic testament. A TESTAMENT, similar to the common law's holographic will, "entirely written, dated, and signed in the handwriting of the TESTATOR." La. C.C. art. 1575.

Testate succession. *See* SUCCESSION, TESTATE SUCCESSION.

Testator. The person making a TESTAMENT.

Theft. In continental legal systems, the "misappropriation or taking of a CORPOREAL MOVABLE, without the consent of its owner, by one who intends to make it his own." La. C.C. art. 521, Comment (b). This definition corresponds to the common law's larceny and undergirds the Louisiana Civil Code's definition of a stolen thing in article 521. *See* THING, STOLEN THING.

Thing.

> **Abandoned thing.** A THING which has been relinquished by its owner, who intends to give up OWNERSHIP. La. C.C. art. 3418.
>
> **Accessory thing.** *Accession.* A "CORPOREAL MOVABLE that serves the use of, ornament[s], or complement[s] ... the PRINCIPAL THING." La. C.C. art. 508.
>
> **Common thing.** THINGS such as air and the high seas that are not susceptible of OWNERSHIP by anyone.
>
> **Consumable thing.** THINGS that cannot be used without being expended, without being consumed, or without their substance being changed. Money, foodstuffs, and beverages are all CONSUMABLES. La. C.C. 536.
>
> **Corporeal thing.** THINGS that have a body, whether animate or inanimate, and can be felt or touched. La. C.C. art. 461. *Contrast* THING, INCORPOREAL THING.
>
> **Immovable thing.** *See* IMMOVABLE.
>
> **Incorporeal thing.** "[T]HINGS that have no body but are comprehended by the understanding, such as the rights of inheritance, SERVITUDES, OBLIGATIONS, and right of intellectual property." La. C.C. art. 461. Similar to intangibles.

Lost thing. A CORPOREAL MOVABLE that has been lost. La. C.C. art. 3419. The finder must make a diligent effort to find the THING'S owner. *Id.* He becomes the owner of the thing if, after diligent effort, three years pass without locating the owner. *Id.*

Movable thing. *See* MOVABLE.

Nonconsumable thing. THINGS that may be used and enjoyed without altering their substance. La. C.C. art. 537. However, "their substance may be diminished or deteriorated naturally by time or by the use to which they are applied, such as lands, houses, shares of stock, animals, furniture, and vehicles." *Id.*

Principal thing. *Accession.* The thing which is served, ornamented, or complemented by an ACCESSORY THING. La. C.C. art. 508.

Private thing. THINGS "owned by individuals, other private persons, and by the state or its political subdivisions in their capacity as a private persons." La. C.C. art. 453.

Public thing. THINGS "owned by the state or its political subdivisions in their capacity as public persons," e.g., navigable water bottoms, the seashore, and public streets. La. C.C. art. 450. Public things are analogous to things in the public domain, public lands, or common property.

Stolen thing. A THING the POSSESSION of which has been taken by someone without the consent of its owner. La. C.C. art. 521. *See* THEFT.

Thing in commerce. A THING that can be bought and sold, *viz.*, a thing that is susceptible of OWNERSHIP the sale of which is not prohibited by law. La. C.C. art. 2448.

Thing not owed. A THING "paid or delivered for discharge of an OBLIGATION that is subject to a SUSPENSIVE CONDITION." La. C.C. art. 2301.

Third person. "With respect to a CONTRACT or judgment, third persons are all who are not parties to it. In case of failure, third persons are, particularly, those creditors of the debtor who contracted with him without knowledge of the rights which he had transferred to another." La. C.C. art. 3506(32).

Third possessor. *Mortgage.* One "who acquires mortgaged property and who is not personally bound for the OBLIGATION the MORTGAGE secures." La. C.C. art. 3315.

Title. A JURIDICAL ACT that gives a person the right to exercise OWNERSHIP or another REAL RIGHT over a THING. *See, e.g.,* La. C.C. art. 3483.

Transferable right. A heritable right. *See* OBLIGATION, HERITABLE OBLIGATION.

Traveler. A PERSON who is "transiently in a place where [he] has no DOMICILE" and who takes his "board and lodging at an inn." La. C.C. art. 3235.

Treasure. A "MOVABLE hidden in another THING, movable or IMMOVABLE, for such a long time that its owner cannot be determined." La. C.C. art. 3420.

Tutor. A person similar to the legal guardian of a child. A female tutor is sometimes called a tutrix.

> **Dative tutor.** A TUTOR appointed by a court.

U

Umpire. A third ARBITRATOR who determines the outcome of the arbitration if the two arbitrators cannot agree. The umpire is either named in the SUBMISSION to arbitrate or selected by the two arbitrators themselves. La. C.C. art. 3116–3117. If the arbitrators cannot agree on the selection of an umpire, he will be appointed by the judge. La. C.C. art. 3118.

Unconditional heir. *Obsolete. See* HEIR, UNCONDITIONAL HEIR.

Undertaker. An artisan who undertakes work by the job, e.g., masons, carpenters, and locksmiths. La. C.C. art. 2771. In modern usage, these workers would be called contractors or tradesmen.

Undue influence. Influence upon a PERSON that so impairs his volition as to have the effect of replacing it with the volition of the person exerting the influence. La. C.C. art. 1479.

Undue influence is very difficult to define and depends very heavily on the circumstances surrounding the alleged influence. *See id.*, Comment (b). "The more subtle influences, such as creating resentment toward a natural object of the TESTATOR's bounty by false statements, may constitute the kind of influence that is reprobated ... but will still call for evaluation by the trier of fact." *Id.*

Unilateral contract. *See* CONTRACT, UNILATERAL CONTRACT.

Unilateral error. *See* ERROR, UNILATERAL ERROR.

Universal legacy. *See* LEGACY, UNIVERSAL LEGACY.

Universal successor. *See* SUCCESSOR, UNIVERSAL SUCCESSOR.

Universal title, legacy under. *Obsolete. See* LEGACY, LEGACY UNDER UNIVERSAL TITLE.

Universal usufruct. *See* USUFRUCT, UNIVERSAL USUFRUCT.

Unjust enrichment. Enrichment not resulting from a valid JURIDICAL ACT or law. La. C.C. art. 2298. "The amount of compensation due if measured by the extent to which one has been enriched or the other has been impoverished, whichever is less." *Id.*

Unlawful case. *See* CAUSE, UNLAWFUL CAUSE.

Unworthiness. The unworthiness of a potential SUCCESSOR to inherit from the decedent's SUCCESSION. "A successor shall be declared unworthy if he is convicted of a crime involving the intentional killing, or attempted killing, of the decedent or is judicially determined to have participated in the intentional, unjustified killing, or attempted killing of the decedent." La. C.C. art. 941.

Use, right of. *See* REAL RIGHT, RIGHT OF USE.

Useful expenses. *See* EXPENSE, USEFUL EXPENSE.

Usufruct. A "REAL RIGHT of limited duration over the property of another." La. C.C. art. 535. The features of this PERSONAL SERVITUDE vary according to the THINGS which are subject to it. *Id.*; *see* USUFRUCT, USUFRUCT OF CONSUMABLES and USUFRUCT OF NONCONSUMABLES.

It is similar to the common law's life estate, although the usufruct need not last for life.

The NAKED OWNER retains the ownership of the property subject to usufruct. Naked ownership is similar to a reversion, estate in reversion, or the residue of a life estate.

> **Conventional usufruct.** A USUFRUCT created by JURIDICAL ACT, either *inter vivos* by CONTRACT or *mortis causa* by TESTAMENT. La. C.C. art. 544, Comment (b).

> **Imperfect usufruct.** *Obsolete.* USUFRUCT OF CONSUMABLES. La. C.C. art. 535, Comment (c).

> **Legal usufruct.** A USUFRUCT established by operation of law, La. C.C. art. 544, e.g., the usufruct in favor of a surviving spouse over her deceased spouse's share of the COMMUNITY PROPERTY not subject to testamentary disposition. *See* La. C.C. art. 890.

> **Perfect usufruct.** *Obsolete.* USUFRUCT OF NONCONSUMABLES. La. C.C. art. 535, Comment (c).

> **Universal usufruct.** The USUFRUCT of an entire SUCCESSION. La. C.C. art. 587.

> **Usufruct in divided portions.** A USUFRUCT that creates a distinct right of enjoyment for each of multiple USUFRUCTUARIES that accrue to the NAKED OWNER as each usufructuary's right terminates. La. C.C. art. 541, Comment (b).

> **Usufruct in undivided portions.** A USUFRUCT that creates a single right apportioned among multiple USUFRUCTUARIES that persists until the termination of the last interest, at which time the right returns to the NAKED OWNER. La. C.C. art. 541, Comment (b).

Usufruct of consumables. A USUFRUCT under which the USUFRUCTUARY becomes owner of the CONSUMABLES and, at the termination of the usufruct, is bound to pay the NAKED OWNER the value of the THINGS at the time of the beginning of the usufruct or to deliver to him things of like quality and quantity. La. C.C. art. 538.

Usufruct of nonconsumables. A USUFRUCT under which the USUFRUCTUARY has the right to possess and enjoy the NONCONSUMABLES as owner. La. C.C. art. 539. The usufructuary owns the CIVIL and NATURAL FRUITS of the THINGS. He is bound to use the things as a PRUDENT ADMIN-ISTRATOR and to return them to the NAKED OWNER at the termination of the usufruct. *Id.*

Usufruct under particular title. The USUFRUCT of individually determined THINGS. La. C.C. art. 587.

Usufruct under universal title. The USUFRUCT of a fraction of a SUCCESSION. La. C.C. art. 587.

Usufructuary. The PERSON entitled to the benefits of a USUFRUCT. Similar to a life tenant.

V

Vacant succession. *See* SUCCESSION, VACANT SUCCESSION.

Vendor's privilege. A PRIVILEGE enjoyed by a seller of MOVABLE or IMMOVABLE property for the sales PRICE over the THINGS sold that remain in the POSSESSION of the buyer. La. C.C. arts. 3227, 3249(1).

Vice.

Vice of consent. ERROR, FRAUD, or duress. La. C.C. art. 1948.

Vice of possession. "POSSESSION that is violent, clandes-tine, discontinuous, or equivocal." La. C.C. art. 3435. *See* POSSESSION.

View and trial. *See* SALE, SALE ON VIEW OR TRIAL.

Vinculum juris. *Latin.* Literally, "bond of law." "The tie that legally binds one person to another; legal bond; OBLIGATION." BLACK'S LAW DICTIONARY 1600 (8th ed. 2004).

Violent possession. *See* POSSESSION, VIOLENT POSSESSION.

Virile portion. *See* VIRILE SHARE.

Virile share. The portion of an OBLIGATION for which each SOLIDARY OBLIGOR is liable. La. C.C. art. 1804. For contractual or quasi-contractual obligations, the obligors' virile shares are equal in the absence of a contrary agreement or judgment. *Id.* On the other hand, the virile share of a tortfeasor is proportionate to his share of the fault. *Id.* Also called the VIRILE PORTION. *See* OBLIGATION, SOLIDARY OBLIGATION.

Voluntary servitude. *See* SERVITUDE, CONVENTIONAL SERVITUDE.

Voyage. A ship's departure and subsequent arrival at another port, its departure and return to the same port when it was at sea for more than sixty days, or its departure on a long journey when more than sixty days have elapsed. La. C.C. art. 3245.

Vulgar substitution. *See* SUBSTITUTION, VULGAR SUBSTITUTION.

W

Warranty of portions. The warranty each coheir owes to the others to guarantee their peaceful possession of the property they inherit against disturbance by any cause existing before the partition of the SUCCESSION. La. C.C. art. 1384.

Whimsical condition. *See* CONDITION, WHIMSICAL CONDITION.

Wildlife. "Wild animals, birds, fish, and shellfish in a state of natural liberty." La. C.C. art. 3413. Wild animals either belong to the state in its capacity as a public person pursuant to legislation or have no owner. *Id.* Wild animals may be tamed or placed in an enclosure, in which case they become the property of their captor. La. C.C. arts. 3415, 3416.

Will. *See* TESTAMENT.

Without cause, enrichment. *See* UNJUST ENRICHMENT.

Writing. *Contracts.* "An ACT UNDER PRIVATE SIGNATURE or an AUTHENTIC ACT." La. C.C. art. 3038, Comment (d).

About the Authors

Gregory W. Rome is a member of Williams & Rome, LLC, a general practice law firm located in Chalmette, Louisiana. His practice areas include family law, successions and estates, property law, business law, and civil litigation. His law firm's website is www.williamsandrome.com, and his email address is gwrome@williamsandrome.com.

Gregory graduated first in his class from Loyola University New Orleans with a Bachelors degree in computer science, and from Tulane Law School with a Juris Doctor degree and a certificate in civil law studies. He is admitted to practice in Louisiana.

While at Tulane, he co-founded the *Civil Law Commentaries*, the first legal journal dedicated to Louisiana law and its historical roots, and served on its inaugural editorial board. He also served as law clerk to the Honorable Kirk A. Vaughn in the 34th Judicial District, State of Louisiana, from 2007 to 2011.

Stephan Kinsella (www.stephankinsella.com) is General Counsel with Applied Optoelectronics, Inc. He is a Senior Fellow with the Ludwig von Mises Institute.

Before joining AOI, Stephan was a partner in the Intellectual Property Department of Duane Morris LLP. He is the author or editor of numerous books and articles about intellectual property law, international law and other topics, including *International Investment, Political Risk, and Dispute Resolution: A Practitioner's Guide* (co-author, Oxford Univ. Press, 2005); *Property, Freedom, and Society: Essays in Honor of Hans-Hermann Hoppe* (co-editor, Mises Institute, 2009); and the journal *Libertarian Papers* (editor, Mises Institute, 2009–present).

Stephan received an LL.M. in international business law from King's College London—University of London, a J.D. from the Louisiana State University Law Center, and MSEE and BSEE degrees from Louisiana State University. He is admitted to practice in Texas, and he is also a member of the bars (inactive) of Louisiana and Pennsylvania.

Visit us at *www.quidprobooks.com*.

www.ingramcontent.com/pod-product-compliance
Lightning Source LLC
Chambersburg PA
CBHW071055280326
41928CB00050B/2518